SWEET BABY BLANKETS TO KNIT

JODY LONG

Tuva Publishing
www.tuvapublishing.com

Address Merkez Mah. Cavusbasi Cad. No:71
Cekmekoy - Istanbul 34782 / Turkey
Tel: +9 0216 642 62 62

Sweet Baby Blankets To Knit

First Print 2017 / September

All Global Copyrights Belong To
Tuva Tekstil ve Yayıncılık Ltd.

Content Knitting

Editor in Chief Ayhan DEMİRPEHLİVAN
Project Editor Kader DEMİRPEHLİVAN
Designer Jody LONG
Technical Editors Leyla ARAS, Büşra ESER
Graphic Designers Ömer ALP, Abdullah BAYRAKÇI, Zilal ÖNEL
Photograph Tuva Publishing

ISBN 978-605-9192-27-9

Printing House
Bilnet Matbaacılık ve Yayıncılık A.Ş.

TuvaYayincilik TuvaPublishing
TuvaYayincilik TuvaPublishing

This book is dedicated to my dearest friend Elaine Gray RGN RM NP who has delivered and wrapped hundreds of babies in hand knitted blankets.

This book would not have been possible without the following people: Tuva Publishing for asking me to write this book, my mum Elaine and sister Kaylie for shipping out yarn to my army of knitters. Sheila Riley, Nikki Ingham, Kay Piper, Valentina Miller, Tina Keogh, Sam Clarke, Pauline Clarke, David Hampshire, Karen Hatton, Paula Paynter, Andrea Brown, Susan Winn, Susan McCarthy and Mary Alderton the amazing knitters who produced extraordinary work under tight deadlines.

Last but not least the amazing team at Tuva Publishing for producing another great book.

INTRODUCTION

I was delighted to be asked to write this book. Designing for babies is one of my favourite things to work on. There is always something special knitting for babies and toddlers, knowing they can be wrapped up warm.

In this book there are 29 blankets, most have instructions for three sizes allowing them to be created for toddlers too. Blankets are always very much appreciated as gifts and make a beautiful present for baby showers.

My favourite is the seed stitch honeycomb entrelac blanket which has a real depth of stitch definition. The blanket could be knitted in any colors to suit the recipient.

Happy Knitting!

Jody Long

CONTENTS

P.82

P.86

P.90

P.94

P.98

P.102

P.106

P.108

P.112

P.116

P.122

P.126

P.128

EQUIPMENTS

The pattern will tell you at the start what equipment is required to knit the project. The most important purchase is that of the knitting needles. These come in a range of diameters, which are either described in metric millimetres or by one of two sizing systems. Check the pattern carefully and if you are unsure, ask in the store before purchasing. However, the pattern will give a suggested size only to achieve the correct number of stitches and rows in a given distance.

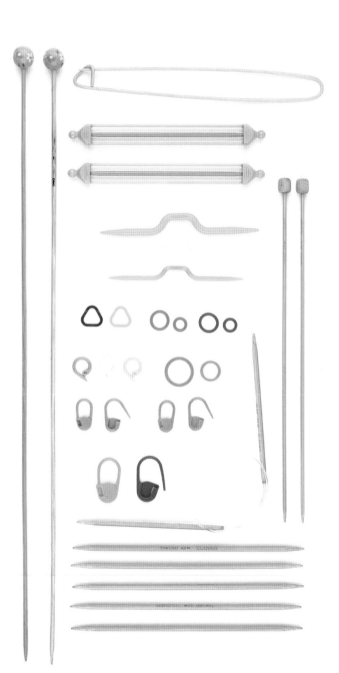

KNITTING NEEDLES
The type used in this book are made from bamboo and are ideal for all types of knitter's because they are light and the stitches are less likely to slide off them than with metal needles.

Check the needles carefully before buying to make sure there is no pitting in the surface and that the points are round and smooth. A longer point is useful on finer sizes. We recommend using Clover knitting needles.

CIRCULAR NEEDLES
Circular needles or "circs" as we lovingly call them, are simply two knitting tips joined by a flexible cord. Use them just as you would straight needles. The big advantage to circular needles is you can knit seamlessly in the round making them perfect for hats, they're much longer too which is great if you need lots of stitches and a straight needle just won't do! We recommend using Clover circular needles.

DOUBLE-POINTED NEEDLES
Double-pointed needles also known as DPNs are pointed at both ends of the needle. They are most useful when working smaller projects like i-cords, hat crowns and socks. Like the circular needles they are great for working in the round and making projects seamless. We recommend using Clover double-pointed needles.

CABLE NEEDLE
This is used for holding stitches to one side while others are being worked within a repeat. Look for a cable needle with a bend in it because it holds the stitches more securely.

STITCH HOLDERS
These prevent stitches from unraveling when not in use. Alternatively, a spare knitting needle of the same size or less (ideally double pointed) can be used as a stitch holder. For holding just a few stitches, a safety pin is always useful.

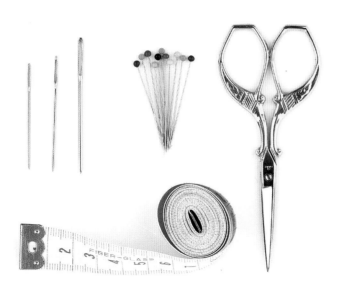

TAPE MEASURE

Useful for greater distances and checking project measurements.

SEWING NEEDLES

These should be blunt and round-pointed with a large eye. A sharp-pointed needle is more likely to split the yarn and/or stitches and result in an uneven seam.

SCISSORS

Always use a nice sharp-pointed pair for easy precise cutting of the yarn.

PINS

Always use large glass/plastic-headed pins so they can be seen and not be left in a knitted garment.

YARN INFORMATION

We have used only natural yarns that are soft and most importantly machine washable.

RULER

A plastic or metal ruler is less likely to become distorted and is useful to check the gauge (tension).

Below you will find all the information about the yarns used within this book, both qualities are available in a large color palette.

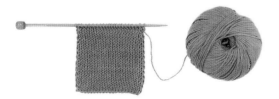

DMC NATURA Just Cotton is a 100% cotton yarn that has a length of 170yd (155m) per 1.75oz (50g) ball.

DMC NATURA JUST COTTON MEDIUM is a 100% cotton yarn that has a length of 82yd (75m) per 1.75oz (50g) ball.

DMC NATURA JUST COTTON XL is a 100% cotton yarn that has a length of 82yd (75m) per 3.5oz (100g) ball.

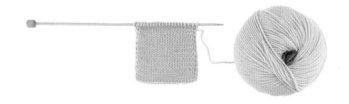

DMC WOOLLY is a natural 100% merino wool yarn that has a length of 136yd (125m) per 1.75oz (50g) ball.

INFORMATION

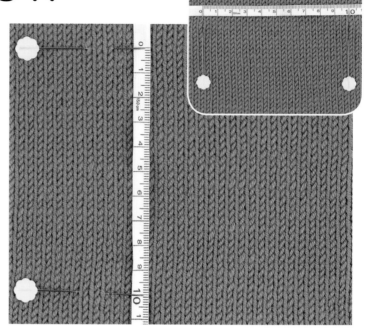

GAUGE (TENSION)

Obtaining the correct tension is perhaps the single factor which can make the difference between a successful garment and a disastrous one. It controls both the shape and size of an article, so any variation, however slight, can distort the finished garment. We recommend that you knit a square in pattern and/ or stockinette (stocking) stitch (depending on the pattern instructions) of perhaps 5 - 10 more stitches and 5 - 10 more rows than those given in the tension note.

Mark out the central 4in (10cm) square with pins. If you have too many stitches to 4in (10cm) try again using thicker needles, if you have too few stitches to 4in (10cm) try again using finer needles.

Once you have achieved the correct tension your garment will be knitted to the measurements indicated in the pattern.

CASTING ON

Although there are many different techniques for casting on stitches, we recommend the long-tail cast on method (see page 15) for details.

STOCKINETTE (STOCKING) STITCH

Alternate one row knit and one row purl. The knit side is the right side of the work unless otherwise stated in the instructions.

GARTER STITCH

Knit every row. Both sides are the same and look identical.

K1, P1 RIB

Alternate one knit stitch with one purl stitch to the end of the row. On the next row, knit all the knit stitches and purl all the purl stitches as they face you.

SEED (MOSS) STITCH

Alternate one knit stitch with one purl stitch to the end of the row. On the next row, knit all the purl stitches and purl and the knit stitches as they face you.

INSTRUCTIONS IN ROUNDED BRACKETS

These are to be repeated the number of times stated after the closing bracket.

INSTRUCTIONS IN SQUARE BRACKETS

The instructions are given for the smallest size just before the opening of the bracket. Where they vary, work the figures in brackets for the larger sizes. One set of figures refer to all sizes.

JOINING YARN

Always join yarn at the beginning of a new row (unless you're working the Fair Isle or Intarsia method), and never knot the yarns as the knot may come through to the right side and spoil your work. Any long loose ends will be useful for sewing up afterwards.

WORKING STRIPES

When knitting different-colored stripes, carry yarns loosely up the side of your work.

FAIR ISLE METHOD

When two or three colors are worked repeatedly across a row, strand the yarn not in use loosely behind the stitches being worked. Always spread the stitches to their correct width to keep them elastic. It is advisable not to carry the stranded or 'floating' yarns over more than three stitches at a time, but weave them under and over the color you are working. The 'floating' yarns are therefore caught at the back of the work.

WORKING A LACE PATTERN

When working a lace pattern it is important to rememberer that if you are unable to work both the increase and corresponding decrease and vice versa, the stitches should be worked in stockinette (stocking) stitch.

WORKING FROM A CHART

Each square on a chart represents a stitch and a line of squares a row of knitting. Alongside the chart there will be a color and/or stitch key. When working from the charts, read odd rows (knit) from right to left and even rows (purl) from left to right, unless otherwise stated.

SEAMS

After working for hours knitting a garment, it seems a great pity that many garments are spoiled because such little care is taken in the pressing and finishing process. Follow the text below for a truly professional-looking garment.

PRESSING

Block out each piece of knitting and following the instructions on the ball band press the garment pieces, omitting the ribs. Tip: Take special care to press the edges, as this will make sewing up both easier and neater. If the ball band indicates that the fabric is not to be pressed, then covering the blocked out fabric with a damp white cotton cloth and leave it to stand will have the desired effect. Darn in all loose ends neatly along the selvage edge or a colour join, as appropriate.

STITCHING

When stitching the pieces together, remember to match areas of color and texture very carefully where they meet. Use a seam stitch such as backstitch or mattress stitch for all main knitting seams and join all ribs and cuffs with mattress stitch, unless otherwise stated.

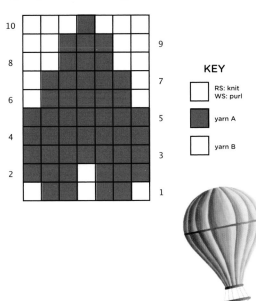

KEY

☐	RS: knit WS: purl
■	yarn A
☐	yarn B

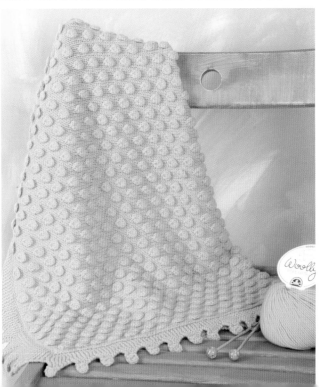

TECHNIQUES

HOLDING THE NEEDLES

Not every knitter holds their needles and yarn in the same way. The yarn can be held in either the right or left hand, the needles can be held from above or below. Try each of the methods described here and work in a way that is most comfortable for you. They are all bound to feel awkward and slow at first.

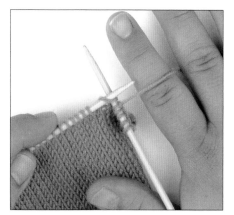

**English method
(yarn in the right hand)**

Left hand: hold the needle with the stitches in your left hand with your thumb lying along the needle, your index finger resting on top near the tip and the remaining fingers curled under the needle to support it. The thumb and the index finger control the stitches and the tip of the needle.

Right hand: pass the yarn over the index finger, under the middle and over the third finger. The yarn lies between the nail and the first joint and the index finger 'throws' the yarn around the right-hand needle when knitting. The yarn should be able to move freely and is tensioned between the middle and third finger. You can wrap the yarn around the little finger if you feel it is too loose and it keeps falling off your fingers. Hold the empty needle in your right hand with

your thumb lying along the needle, your index finger near the tip and the remaining fingers curled under the needle to support it (see right hand in Continental method).

Some knitters prefer to hold the end of the right-hand needle under their right arm, anchoring it firmly. Whilst knitting this needle remains still and the right hand is above the needle and moves the yarn around it.

Alternative grip

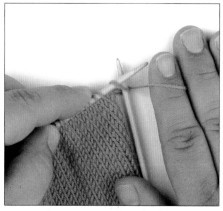

Left hand: hold the needle in the same way as shown above left.

Right hand: hold the yarn in the fingers the same way as shown above. Hold the needle like a pen, on top of the hand between thumb and index finger. The end of the needle will be above your right arm, in the crook of the elbow. As the fabric grows longer, the thumb will hold the needle behind the knitting.

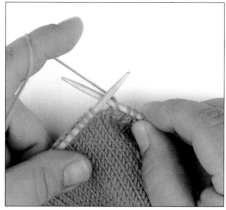

**Continental method
(yarn in the left hand)**

Left hand: wrap the yarn around your little finger, under the middle two fingers and then over the index finger between the nail and the first joint. The yarn is held taut between the index finger and the needle. Hold the needle with your thumb lying along the needle, your index finger near the tip and remaining fingers curled under the needle to support it. The thumb and index finger control the stitches, yarn and needle tip.

Right hand: hold the empty needle in your right hand with your thumb lying along the needle, index finger resting on top near the tip and remaining fingers curled under the needle to support it. The thumb and index finger control the stitches and the needle tip, which hooks the yarn and draws the loop through.

To begin knitting, you need to work a foundation row of stitches called casting on. There are several ways to cast on depending on the type of edge that you want. The cast on edge should be firm; too loose and it will look untidy and flare out, too tight and it will break and the stitches unravel. If your casting on is always too tight, use a size larger needle. If it is always too loose, use a size smaller needle. Remember to change back to the correct size needle to begin knitting.

Thumb method
This is the simplest way of casting on and you will need only one needle.

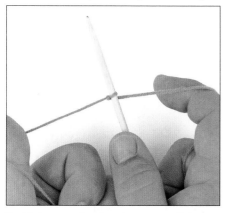

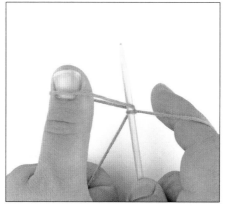

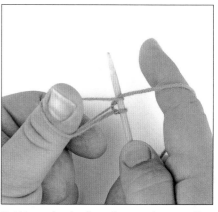

1. Make a slip knot some distance from the end of the yarn (see Knit Perfect) and place it on the needle. Hold the needle in your right hand. Pass the ball end of the yarn over the index finger, under the middle and then over the third finger. Holding the free end of yarn in your left hand, wrap it around your left thumb from front to back.

2. Insert the needle through the thumb loop from front to back.

3. Wrap the ball end over the needle.

The slip knot counts as the first cast on stitch. It is made some distance from the end of the yarn and placed on the needle. Pull the ends of the yarn to tighten it. You now have two ends of yarn coming from the slip knot; the ball end attached to the ball and a shorter free end.

For the thumb method of casting on, you will need approximately 1in (2.5cm) for every stitch you want to cast on. When you have cast on, you should have at least a 6in (15cm) length to sew in.

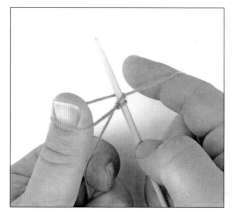

4. Pull a new loop through the thumb loop by passing the thumb loop over the end of the needle. Remove your thumb and tighten the new loop on the needle by pulling the free end. Continue in this way until you have cast on the required number of stitches.

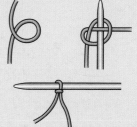

INTRODUCING KNIT STITCH

In knitting there are only two stitches to learn - knit stitch (K) and purl stitch (P). They are the foundation of all knitted fabrics. Once you have mastered these two simple stitches, by combining them in different ways you will soon be knitting ribs, textures, cables and many more exciting fabrics.

English Method (yarn in the right hand)
In knit stitch the yarn is held at the back of the work (the side facing away from you) and is made up of four steps.

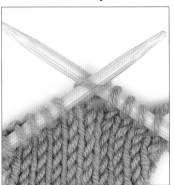

1. Hold the needle with the cast on stitches in your left hand, and insert the right-hand needle into the front of the stitch from left to right.

2. Pass the yarn under and around the right-hand needle.

3. Pull the new loop on the right-hand needle through the stitch on the left-hand needle.

4. Slip the stitch off the left-hand needle. One knit stitch is completed.

To continue...
Repeat these four steps for each stitch on the left-hand needle. All the stitches on the left-hand needle will be transferred to the right-hand needle where the new row is formed. At the end of the row, swap the needle with the stitches into your left hand and the empty needle into your right hand, and work the next row in the same way.

BINDING (CASTING) OFF

1. Knit two stitches, insert the tip of left-hand needle into the front of the first stitch on the right-hand needle. Lift this stitch over the second stitch and off the needle.

2. One stitch is left on the right-hand needle. Knit the next stitch and lift the second stitch over this and off the needle. Continue in this way until one stitch remains on the right-hand needle.

3. To finish, cut the yarn (leaving a length long enough to sew in), thread the end through the last stitch and slip it off the needle. Pull the yarn end to tighten the stitch and secure.

Bind (cast) off purlwise
To bind (cast) off on a purl row, simply purl the stitches instead of knitting them.

You may find purl stitch a little harder to learn than knit stitch. But really it is just the reverse of a knit stitch. If you purled every row, you would produce garter stitch (the same as if you knitted every row). It is not often that you will work every row in purl stitch; it is easier and faster to knit every row if you want garter stitch.

English method (yarn in the right hand)
In purl stitch the yarn is held at the front of the work (the side facing you) and is made up of four steps.

1. Hold the needle with the cast on stitches in your left hand, and insert the right-hand needle into the front of the stitch from right to left.

2. Pass the yarn over and around the right-hand needle.

3. Pull the new loop on the right-hand needle through the stitch on the left-hand needle.

4. Slip the stitch off the left-hand needle. One stitch is completed.

To continue...
Repeat these four steps for each stitch on the left-hand needle. All the stitches on the left-hand needle will be transferred to the right-hand needle where the new purl row is formed. At the end of the row, swap the needle with the stitches into your left hand and the empty needle into your right hand, and work the next row in the same way.

To shape knitting, stitches are increased or decreased. Increases are used to make a piece of knitting wider by adding more stitches, either on the ends of rows or within the knitting.

Some increases are worked to be invisible whilst others a meant to be seen and are known as decorative increase You can increase one stitch at a time or two or more.

Increasing one stitch

The easiest way to increase one stitch is to work into the front and back of the same stitch. This produces a small bar across the second (increase) satitch and is very visible. This makes counting the increases easier.

On a knit row (Kfb)

1. Knit into the front of the stitch as usual, do not slip the stitch off the left-hand needle but knit into it again through the back of the loop.

2. Slip the original stitch off the left-hand needle. You have now increased an extra stitch and you can see the bar (increased stitch) to the left of the original stitch.

On a purl row (Pfb)

3. Purl into the front of the stitch as usual, do not slip the stitch off the left-hand needle but purl into it again through the back of the loop.

4. Slip the original stitch off the left-hand needle. You have now increased an extra stitch and you can see the bar (increased stitch) to the left of the original stitch.

To make a neater edge when working increases at the beginning and end of rows, work the increase stitches a few stitches from the end. This leaves a continuous stitch up the edge of the fabric that makes sewing up easier. Because the made stitch lies to the left of the original stitch, at the beginning of a knit row you knit one stitch, then make the increase, but at the end of a knit row you work the increase into the third stitch from the end. The increase stitch lies between the second and third stitches at each end.

On a purl row you work in exactly the same way; the bar will be in the correct position two stitches from either end.

MAKE 1

This is another way to increase one stitch and is often used where increasing stitches after a rib. The new stitch is made between two existing stitches using the horizontal thread that lies between the stitches - called the running thread. This is an invisible increase and is harder to see when counting.

On a knit row (M1)

1. Knit to the point where the increase is to be made. Insert the tip of the left-hand needle under the running thread from front to back.

2. Knit this loop through the back to twist it. By twisting the stitch it will prevent leaving a hole appearing where the made stitch is.

On a purl row (M1P)

To work this increase on a purl row, work as given for the knit way but instead purl into the back of the loop.

Increasing more than one stitch

To increase two stitches simply knit into the front, back and then the front again of the same stitch. When knitting bobbles, you will sometimes make five, six or seven stitches out of one stitch in this way. For example, to make seven stitches the instructions would read (k into front and back of same st) 3 times, then k into front again.

MATTRESS STITCH

This technique produces a discreet seam that is especially good if the edge stitches are not very neat, as they become part of the seam inside the project. The other advantage of mattress stitch is that it is worked from the right side of work, so the neatness of the seam can be assessed as the seam is stitched and adjustments made immediately, rather than having to painstakingly unpick the whole seam. Careful preparation will pay dividends, so press and block the pieces first if required, paying particular attention to the edge stitches. Then pin the seams together and matching pattern if there is any to be matched.

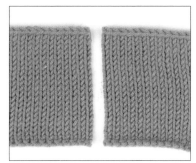

1. Place the edges that need seaming together with right sides of work facing you.

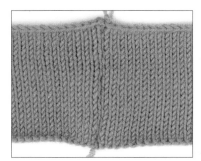

3. The neatest seam is achieved by pulling the yarn just enough to pull the stitches together.

2. Working from the bottom, and between the first and second stitch in from the edge, pass the needle under the loops of two rows on one side; then pass the needle under the loops of the corresponding two rows on other side. Work a few stitches like this before drawing the first stitches tight as this will help to keep track of the line of the seam.

17

Decreasing is used at the ends of rows or within the knitted fabric to reduce the number of stitches being worked on. This means that you can shape your knitted fabric by making it narrower.

Decreasing one stitch

The simplest way to decrease one stitch is to knit or purl two stitches together (K2tog or P2tog). Both of these methods produce the same result on the front (knit side) of the work; the decrease slopes to the right.

(K2tog or P2tog). Both of these methods produce the same result on the front (knit side) of the work; the decrease slopes to the right.

P2tog on a p row Purl to where the decrease is to be, insert the right-hand needle (as though to purl) through the next two stitches and purl them together as one stitch.

Always read how to work a decrease very carefully. Some of them have similar abbreviations with only a slight difference between them.

In patterns the designer may use different abbreviations to those given here. Always check the detailed explanation of abbreviations.

K2tog tbl on a k row Knit to where the decrease is to be, insert the right-hand needle through the back of the next two stitches and knit them together as one stitch.

P2tog tbl on a p row Purl to where the decrease is to be, insert the right-hand needle through the back of the next two stitches and purl them together as one stitch.

Decorative decreasing one stitch purlwise

Sometimes decreases are decorative, especially in lace knitting where they form part of the pattern. Then you have to be aware of whether the decrease slants right or left. Each decrease has an opposite and the two of them are called a pair. There is one way to work the decrease that is the pair to p2tog which slopes to the left when seen on the front (knit side) of the work.

There are two ways to work the decrease that is the pair to K2tog. They both produce the same result and slope to the left.

Slip one, slip one, knit two together (SSK)

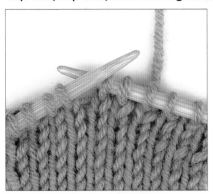

1. Slip two stitches knitwise one at a time from left-hand needle to right-hand needle.

2. Insert the left-hand needle from left to right through the fronts of these two stitches and knit together as one stitch.

Slip one, knit one, pass slipped stitch over (SKPO)

1. Insert the right-hand needle knitwise into the next stitch.

2. Slip it on to the right-hand needle without knitting it, then knit the next stitch.

3. With the tip of the left-hand needle, lift the slipped stitch over the knitted stitch and off the needle. This is like binding (casting) off one stitch.

Slip two, knit one, pass the two slipped stitches over (SK2PO)

1. Insert the right-hand needle knitwise into the next two stitches as if to knit two stitches together without knitting them, slip the two stitches from left-hand needle to right-hand needle.

2. Knit the next stitch, then with the tip of left-hand needle, lift the two slipped stitches over the knitted stitch and off the needle.

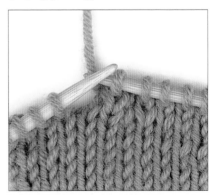

3. You have now completed the central double decrease.

GARTER STITCH

Knit every row

When you knit every row the fabric you make is called garter stitch (g st) and has rows of raised ridges on the front and back of the fabric. It looks the same on the back and the front so it is reversible. Garter stitch lies flat, is quite a thick fabric and does not curl at the edges. These qualities make it ideal for borders and collars, as well as for scarves and the main fabric of a garment.

CABLES

Cable knitting always looks more difficult then it actual is. It is simply done by using a cable needle (third needle) to temporarily hold stitches to be transferred to the front or back of your work. Always remember if the cable needle is at the back of work then the cable will lean to the right. If the cable needle is at the front of work then the cable will lean to the left. There are many different cables, always read the instructions and abbreviations carefully as they may look alike or other designers may use different abbreviations. The number of stitches to be moved will be stated in the pattern. Normally cables are worked only on the right side of work, however I have been known to design garments with cables on the wrong side of work too.

Cable front

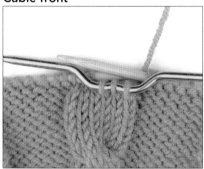 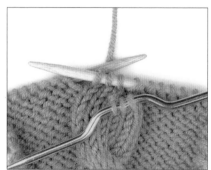 

1. Put the number of stitches stated onto a cable needle.

2. Position the cable needle at the front of the work and knit or purl the stated number of stitches from the left-hand needle.

3. Then knit or purl the stated number of stitches from the cable needle.

Cable back

Cable back differs only in that the stitches slipped onto the cable needle are held at the back of the work while the stitches are knitted or purled from the left-hand needle.

Seed (Moss) stitch

Alternate one knit stitch with one purl stitch to the end of the row. On the next row, knit all the purl stitches and purl and the knit stitches as they face you.

1x1 RIB

Alternate one knit stitch with one purl stitch to the end of the row. On the next row, knit all the knit stitches and purl all the purl stitches as they face you.

LACE

Simple lace is made up of yarn overs to make a stitch with a pairing decrease to keep the stitch count the same on each row. More complicated lace may have variable stitch counts. No matter which one you are working the rules are the same; If you do not have enough stitches to decrease a yarn over then work this stitch plain and vice versa.

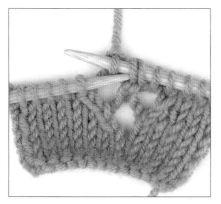

1. Knit to where the pattern states and work a yarn over, by taking the yarn under and over the needle to create a stitch.

2. Work the next two stitches together and work to the end of the row.

3. After working several rows of lace pattern it becomes easier to follow your knitting.

INTARSIA

Intarsia is a technique of color knitting used when the color forms blocks within a design. The word intarsia describes the method of securing the blocks of color together. It forms a single layer fabric, which means it is economical with yarn and has a drop similar to a single color fabric. (see page 11) on how to read a chart.

1. Using the color stated in the pattern knit to where the color needs to be changed. Then insert the right-hand needle into the next stitch, and pass the new color under the last color before working the next stitch.

2. The technique is exactly the same for a purl row. The reason you must twisting the yarn colors together as they meet is to avoid leaving a hole.

3. When working a straight color change you will notice you have colored vertical lines on the wrong side of your knitting if you are working the intarsia method correctly. If you work a diagonal color change the colored line where the yarns meet will also run diagonally.

PROJECTS

SQUARE LEAF BLANKET

SIZE
Width (approx): 31½ in (80 cm)
Length (approx): 31½ in (80 cm)

ABBREVIATIONS
See inside front flap

SPECIAL ABBREVIATION
MB knit into front and back then front again of next st, turn, P3, turn, K3, turn, P1, P2tog, turn, K2tog.

MATERIALS NEEDED
• **DMC Woolly** (136 yd/125 m per 50g ball)
10 x balls of Pink (042)
• US 5 (3.75 mm) needles

GAUGE (TENSION)
25 sts and 32 rows to 4 in (10 cm) measured over st st using US 5 (3.75 mm) needles.

SMALL SQUARES (make 16)

Using US 5 (3.75 mm) needles CO 3 sts.

Row 1 (RS): Kfb, K2. 4 sts.

Row 2: Kfb, P1, K2. 5 sts.

Row 3: Kfb, K1, yo, K1, yo, K2. 8 sts.

Row 4: Kfb, K1, P3, K3. 9 sts.

Row 5: Kfb, K3, yo, K1, yo, K4. 12 sts.

Row 6: Kfb, K2, P5, K4. 13 sts.

Row 7: Kfb, K5, yo, K1, yo, K6. 16 sts.

Row 8: Kfb, K3, P7, K5. 17 sts.

Row 9: Kfb, K7, yo, K1, yo, K8. 20 sts.

Row 10: Kfb, K4, P9, K6. 21 sts.

Row 11: Kfb, K9, yo, K1, yo, K10. 24 sts.

Row 12: Kfb, K5, P11, K7. 25 sts.

Row 13: Kfb, K11, yo, K1, yo, K12. 28 sts.

Row 14: Kfb, K6, P13, K8. 29 sts.

Row 15: Kfb, K7, skpo, K9, K2tog, K8. 28 sts.

Row 16: Kfb, K7, P11, K9. 29 sts.

Row 17: Kfb, K8, skpo, K7, K2tog, K9. 28 sts.

Row 18: Kfb, K8, P9, K10. 29 sts.

Row 19: Kfb, K9, skpo, K5, K2tog, K10. 28 sts.

Row 20: Kfb, K9, P7, K11. 29 sts.

Row 21: Kfb, K10, skpo, K3, K2tog, K11. 28 sts.

Row 22: Kfb, K10, P5, K12. 29 sts.

Row 23: Kfb, K11, skpo, K1, K2tog, K12. 28 sts.

Row 24: Kfb, K11, P3, K13. 29 sts.

Row 25: Kfb, K12, slip next 2 sts as though to K2tog, K1, then pass the 2 slipped sts over, K13. 28 sts.

Rows 26 and 27: Kfb, K to end.

Row 28: Pfb, P to end. 31 sts.

Rows 29 and 30: As rows 26 and 27.

Row 31: Kfb, K1, *yo, K2tog, rep from * to last st, K1. Rep rows 26 to 31 twice more, then rows 26 to 28 once more. 49 sts.

Row 47: Kfb, K3, *K2tog, yo, K1, yo, skpo, K4, rep from * to end. 50 sts.

Rows 48 and 50: Pfb, P to end.

Row 49: Kfb, K3, *K2tog, yo, K3, yo, skpo, K2, rep from * to last 2 sts, K2. 52 sts.

Row 51: Kfb, K3, *K2tog, yo, K2, MB, K2, yo, skpo, rep from * to last 4 sts, K4. 54 sts.

Row 52: Pfb, P to end. 55 sts. (Place a colored thread at each end to mark the corner of the square. The square now begins to decrea-se).

Row 53: Skpo, K4, *yo, skpo, K3, K2tog, yo, K2, rep from * to last 4 sts, K2, K2tog. 53 sts.

Rows 54 and 56: Purl.

Row 55: Skpo, *K4, yo, skpo, K1, K2tog, yo, rep from * to last 6 sts, K4, K2tog. 51 sts.

Row 57: Skpo, *K4, yo, sl 1, K2tog, psso, yo, K2, rep from * to last 4 sts, K2, K2tog. 49 sts.

Row 58: Purl.

Row 59: Skpo, K to last 2 sts, K2tog.

Rows 60 and 62: Knit.

Row 61: Skpo, K1, *yo, K2tog, rep from * to last 2 sts, K2tog.

Row 63: Skpo, K to last 2 sts, K2tog. Rep rows 58 to 63 twice more, then row 58 once more. 31 sts.

Row 77: Skpo, *K5, MB, K2, rep from * to last 5 sts, K3, K2tog. 29 sts.

Row 78 and every foll alt row: Purl.

Row 79: Skpo, K to last 2 sts, K2tog. 27 sts.

Row 81: Skpo, K1, MB, *K3, MB, rep from * to last 3 sts, K1, K2tog. 25 sts.

Row 83: Skpo, K to last 2 sts, K2tog. 23 sts.

Row 85: Skpo, K1, MB, *K7, MB, rep from * to last 3 sts, K1, K2tog. 21 sts.

Row 86: Purl.

Row 87: Skpo, K to last 2 sts, K2tog.

Rows 88 and 90: Knit.

Row 89: Skpo, K1, *yo, K2tog, rep from * to last 2 sts, K2tog.

Row 91: Skpo, K to last 2 sts, K2tog.

Row 92: Purl. Rep rows 87 to 92 twice more. 3 sts.

Row 105: Sl 1, K2tog, psso. 1 st. Cut off yarn and fasten off rem st securely.

FINISHING

Block each square to measure 7.5 in (19 cm), making sure the corners are square. Join four small squares together using backstitch or mattress stitch if preferred to make one big square with large leaves meeting in the middle, then join the big squares together as shown in diagram below.

BORDER

Using US 5 (3.75 mm) needles CO 6 sts.

Row 1 (RS): K3, yo, K1, yo, K2. 8 sts.

Row 2: P6, Kfb, K1. 9 sts.

Row 3: K2, P1, K2, yo, K1, yo, K3. 11 sts.

Row 4: P8, Kfb, K2. 12 sts.

Row 5: K2, P2, K3, yo, K1, yo, K4. 14 sts.

Row 6: P10, Kfb, K3. 15 sts.

Row 7: K2, P3, skpo, K5, K2tog, K1. 13 sts.

Row 8: P8, Kfb, P1, K3. 14 sts.

Row 9: K2, P1, K1, P2, skpo, K3, K2tog, K1. 12 sts.

Row 10: P6, Kfb, K1, P1, K3. 13 sts.

Row 11: K2, P1, K1, P3, skpo, K1, K2tog, K1. 11 sts.

Row 12: P4, Kfb, K2, P1, K3. 12 sts.

Row 13: K2, P1, K1, P4, sl 1, K2tog, psso, K1. 10 sts.

Row 14: P2tog, BO 3 sts knitwise (1 st on right needle), K1, P1, K3. 6 sts.
These 14 rows form patt.

Cont in patt until straight edge of border fits along outer edge of blanket (sewing as you go), easing around corners and ending with row 13 and facing for next row.

Next row (WS): P2tog, BO 8 sts in patt.

FINISHING

Join remainder of border to blanket edge, then join CO and BO edges together.

• Diagram for sewing the 4 large squares together.

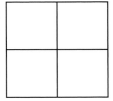

LOVE HEART BLANKET

SIZE
Width (approx): 23½ [28: 32¼] in (59.5 [71: 82] cm)
Length (approx): 30 [35: 40] in (76 [89: 102] cm)

ABBREVIATIONS
See inside front flap

MATERIALS NEEDED
- **DMC Woolly** (136 yd/125 m per 50g ball)
6 [9: 12] x balls of Bright Pink (054)
- US 5 (3.75 mm) needles

GAUGE (TENSION)
25 sts and 32 rows to 4 in (10 cm) measured over st st using US 5 (3.75 mm) needles.

BLANKET

Using US 5 (3.75 mm) needles CO 149 [177: 205] sts.
Work in g st for 16 [18: 20] rows, ending with RS facing for next row.

Next row (RS): K10 [11: 12], work next 129 [155: 181] sts as row 1 of chart as folls, beg and ending rows as indicated and repeating the 26 st patt rep section in red 4 [5: 6] times across row, K10 [11: 12].
Last row set the sts - central 129 [155: 181] sts in patt from chart with 10 [11: 12] edge sts either side in g st for border.
Keeping patt correct and starting with row 2 of chart, cont as set until all 76 rows of chart has been completed 3 [3: 4] times in total, then work rows 1-38, 0 [1: 0] times, ending with RS facing for next row.
Work in g st for 16 [18: 20] rows, ending with RS facing for next row.
BO.

FINISHING

Block to measurements carefully following instructions on ball band.

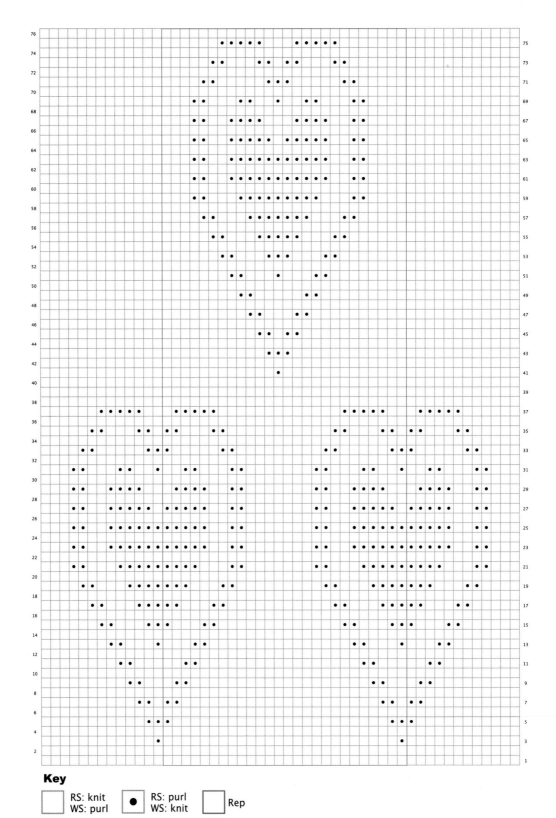

Key

| | RS: knit
WS: purl | ● | RS: purl
WS: knit | | Rep |

30

31

LACY LEAVES BLANKET

SIZE

Width (approx): 24¼ [27: 30¼] in (62 [69: 77] cm)
Length (approx): 31½ [35½: 39½] in (80 [90: 100] cm)

ABBREVIATIONS

See inside front flap

MATERIALS NEEDED

• **DMC Woolly** (136 yd/125 m per 50g ball)
5 [6: 7] x balls of Avocado (084)
• US 3 (3.25 mm) needles
• US 6 (4 mm) needles

GAUGE (TENSION)

23.5 sts and 28 rows to 4 in (10 cm) measured over patt using US 6 (4 mm) needles.

BLANKET

Using US 6 (4 mm) needles CO 145 [163: 181] sts.

Row 1 (RS): *P1, K4, K3tog, yo, K1, yo, P1, yo, K1, yo, sl 1, K2tog, psso, K4, rep from * to last st, P1.

Row 2 and every foll alt row: *K1, P8, rep from * to last st, K1.

Row 3: *P1, K2, K3tog, (K1, yo) twice, K1, P1, K1, (yo, K1) twice, sl 1, K2tog, psso, K2, rep from * to last st, P1.

Row 5: *P1, K3tog, K2, yo, K1, yo, K2, P1, K2, yo, K1, yo, K2, sl 1, K2tog, psso, rep from * to last st, P1.

Row 6: As row 2.
These 6 rows form patt.

Cont in patt until work meas approx 30 [33 ¾ : 37 ½] in (76.5 [86: 95.5] cm), ending with row 6 and RS facing for next row. Change to US 3 (3.25 mm) needles.
Work in g st for 16 [18: 20] rows, ending with RS facing for next row.
BO.

FINISHING

Block to measurements carefully following instructions on ball band.

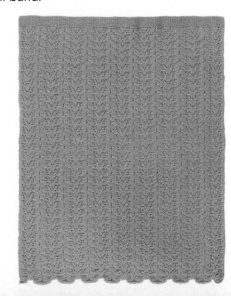

BOBBLE BLANKET

SIZE
Width (approx): 25½ [29½: 33½] in (65 [75: 85] cm)
Length (approx): 25½ [29½: 33½] in (65 [75: 85] cm)

ABBREVIATIONS
See inside front flap

SPECIAL ABBREVIATION
MB knit into front, back, front, back then front again of next st, turn, P5, turn, K5, turn, P2tog, P1, P2tog, turn, sl 1, K2tog, psso.

MATERIALS NEEDED
• **DMC Woolly** (136 yd/125 m per 50g ball)
8 [10: 12] x balls of Yellow (093)
• US 6 (4 mm) needles

GAUGE (TENSION)
23 sts and 28 rows to 4 in (10 cm) measured over patt using US 6 (4 mm) needles.

BLANKET

Using US 6 (4 mm) needles CO 135 [159: 183] sts.

Row 1 (RS): Knit.

Row 2 and every foll alt row: Purl.

Row 3: K3, MB, *K7, MB, rep from * to last 3 sts, K3.

Row 5: As row 1.

Row 7: K7, *MB, K7, rep from * to end.

Row 8: Purl.
These 8 rows form patt.
Contin patt until work meas approx 23 [27: 31] in (59 [69: 79] cm), ending with row 8 of patt and RS facing for next row. BO.

FINISHING

Block to measurements carefully following instructions on ball band.

BORDER

Using US 6 (4 mm) needles CO 5 sts.

Row 1 (RS): K3, Kfb, K1. 6 sts.

Row 2 and every foll alt row: Knit.

Row 3: K4, Kfb, K1. 7 sts.

Row 5: K5, Kfb, K1. 8 sts.

Row 7: K6, Kfb, K1. 9 sts.

Row 9: K7, Kfb, K1. 10 sts.

Row 11: K8, Kfb, MB. 11 sts.

Row 12: BO 6 sts (1 st on right needle) K to end. 5 sts. These 12 rows form patt.

Cont in patt until straight edge of border fits along outer edge of blanket (sewing as you go), easing around corners and ending with row 11 and **WS** facing for next row.
BO knitwise (on **WS**).
Join remainder of border to blanket edge, then join CO and BO edges together.

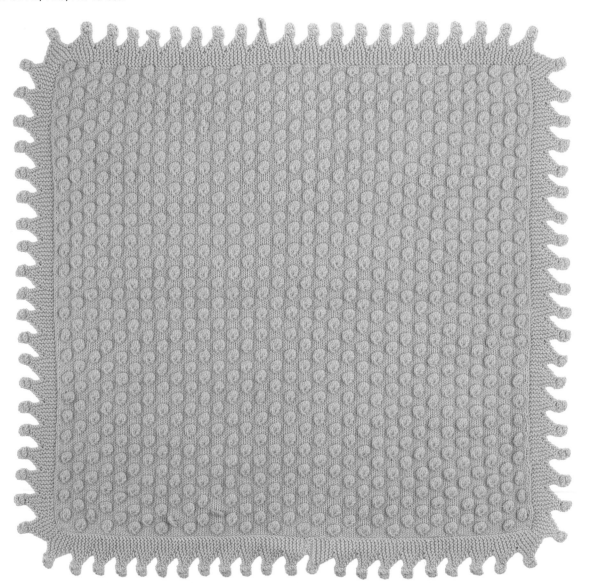

SAMPLER BLANKET

SIZE
Width (approx): 26 [31½: 37¼] in (66.5 [80.5: 94.5] cm)
Length (approx): 35 [40½: 45½] in (89 [103: 116] cm)

ABBREVIATIONS
See inside front flap

SPECIAL ABBREVIATION
MB knit into front and back then front again of next st, turn, P3, turn, K3, turn, P3, turn, sl 1, K2tog, psso.

MATERIALS NEEDED
DMC Woolly (136 yd/125 m per 50g ball)
7 [9: 11] x balls of Cream (003)
US 5 (3.75 mm) needles
US 6 (4 mm) needles

GAUGE (TENSION)
23 sts and 28 rows to 4 in (10 cm) measured over st st using US 6 (4 mm) needles.

BLANKET

Using US 5 (3.75 mm) needles CO 153 [185: 217] sts.
Work in g st for 16 [18: 20] rows, ending with RS facing for next row.

Change to US 6 (4 mm) needles.

Next row (RS): K10 [11: 12], work next 133 [163: 193] sts as row 1 of chart as folls, beg and ending rows as indicated and repeating the 30 st rep section in red 4 [5: 6] times across row, K10 [11: 12].

Last row set the sts - central 133 [163: 193] sts in patt from chart with 10 [11: 12] edge sts either side in g st for border.
Keeping patt correct and starting with row 2 of chart, cont as set until all 36 rows of chart has been completed 6 [7: 8] times in total then work rows 1 to 14 once more, ending with RS facing for next row.

Change to US 5 (3.75 mm) needles.
Work in g st for 16 [18: 20] rows, ending with RS facing for next row.
BO.

FINISHING

Block to measurements carefully following instructions on ball band.

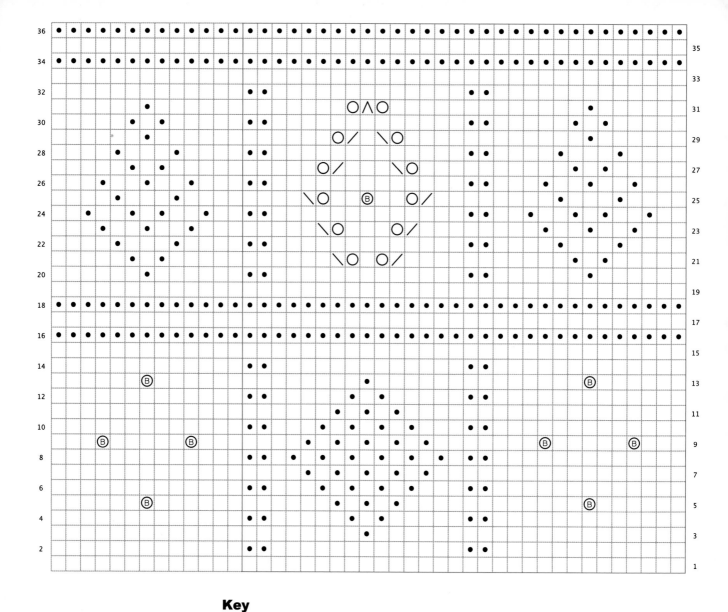

Key

	RS: knit / WS: purl		Skpo
	RS: purl / WS: knit (•)		sl1, k2tog, psso
	yo (O)		Make bobble (B)
	K2tog (/)		Rep

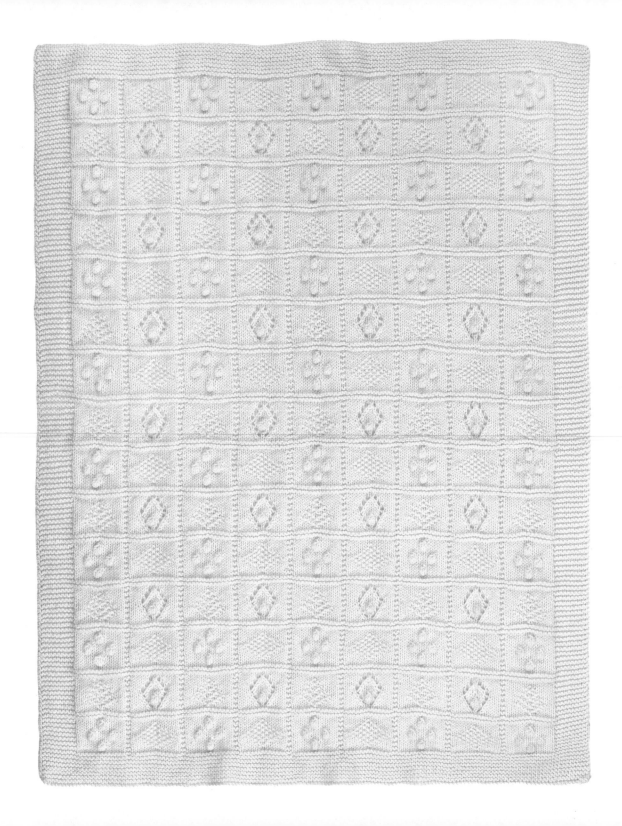

STARS AND DIAMOND BLANKET

SIZE

Width (approx): 20½ [25½: 31½] in (52 [65: 80] cm)
Length (approx): 28¼ [31½: 35½] in (72 [80: 90] cm)

ABBREVIATIONS

See inside front flap

MATERIALS NEEDED

- **DMC Woolly** (136 yd/125 m per 50g ball)
6 [7: 9] x balls of Duck Egg (073)
- US 5 (3.75 mm) needles

GAUGE (TENSION)

24 sts and 40 rows to 4 in (10 cm) measured over patt using US 5 (3.75 mm) needles.

BLANKET

Using US 5 (3.75 mm) needles CO 125 [157: 193] sts.

Row 1 (RS): P1, *K1, P1, rep from * to end.
The last row forms seed (moss) st.
Cont in seed (moss) st for a further 23 [23: 25] rows, ending with RS facing for next row.

Next row (RS): (P1, K1) 7 [7: 8] times, work next 97 [129: 161] sts as row 1 of chart as folls, beg and ending rows as indicated and repeating the 32 st rep section in red 3 [4: 5] times across row, (K1, P1) 7 [7: 8] times.
Last row set the sts - central 97 [129: 161] sts in patt from chart with 14 [14: 16] edge sts either side in seed (moss) st for border.
Keeping patt correct and starting with row 2 of chart, cont as set until all 32 rows of chart has been completed 8 [9: 10] times in total, ending with RS facing for next row.

Row 1 (RS): P1, *K1, P1, rep from * to end.
The last row forms seed (moss) st.
Cont in seed (moss) st for a further 23 [23: 25] rows, ending with RS facing for next row.
BO in patt.

FINISHING

Block to measurements carefully following instructions on ball band.

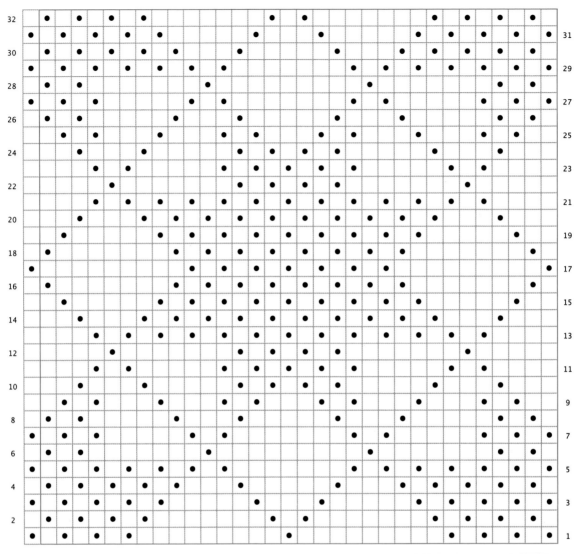

Key

☐ RS: knit WS: purl	● RS: purl WS: knit	☐ Rep

STRIPED BLANKET WITH POMPOMS

SIZE
Width (approx): 24 [28: 32] in (61 [71: 81] cm)
Length (approx): 24 [28: 32] in (61 [71: 81] cm)

ABBREVIATIONS
See inside front flap

MATERIALS NEEDED
• **DMC Woolly** (136 yd/125 m per 50g ball)
4 [5: 6] x balls of Beige (110) **A**
2 [3: 3] x balls of Cream (003) **B**
• US 3 (3.25 mm) needles
• US 6 (4 mm) needles

GAUGE (TENSION)
23 sts and 28 rows to 4 in (10 cm) measured over st st using US 6 (4 mm) needles.

STRIPE SEQUENCE
Rows 1 and 2: Using yarn **A**.
Rows 3 and 4: Using yarn **B**.
These 4 rows form stripe sequence.

BLANKET

Using US 6 (4 mm) needles and yarn CO 117 [140: 163] sts.
Beg with a K row and stripe row 1, work in st st in stripe sequence (see left column) as folls:

Cont straight until work meas approx 20 [24: 28] in (51 [61: 71] cm), ending with row 2 of stripe sequence and RS facing for next row.
BO using yarn **A**.

BOTTOM AND TOP BORDERS (both alike)

With RS facing, using US 3 (3.25 mm) needles and yarn **A,** pick up and knit 140 [164: 188] sts evenly along CO or BO edge.

Next row (WS): Knit.

Row 1 (RS): K3, P2, *K2, P2, rep from * to last 3 sts, K3.

Row 2: K1, P2, *K2, P2, rep from * to last st, K1.
These 2 rows form rib.
Cont in rib for a further 16 rows, ending with RS facing for next row.
BO in rib.

SIDE BORDERS (both alike)

With RS facing, using US 3 (3.25 mm) needles and yarn **A,** pick up and knit 15 sts evenly along border, 146 [174: 202] sts evenly along side edge of blanket and 15 sts evenly along border. 176 [204: 232] sts.

Next row (WS): Knit.

Row 1 (RS): K3, P2, *K2, P2, rep from * to last 3 sts, K3.

Row 2: K1, P2, *K2, P2, rep from * to last st, K1. These 2 rows form rib. Cont in rib for a further 16 rows, ending with RS facing for next row.
BO in rib.

FINISHING

Block to measurements carefully following instructions on ball band. Make four 2 in (5 cm) pompoms and attach to each corner of blanket border.

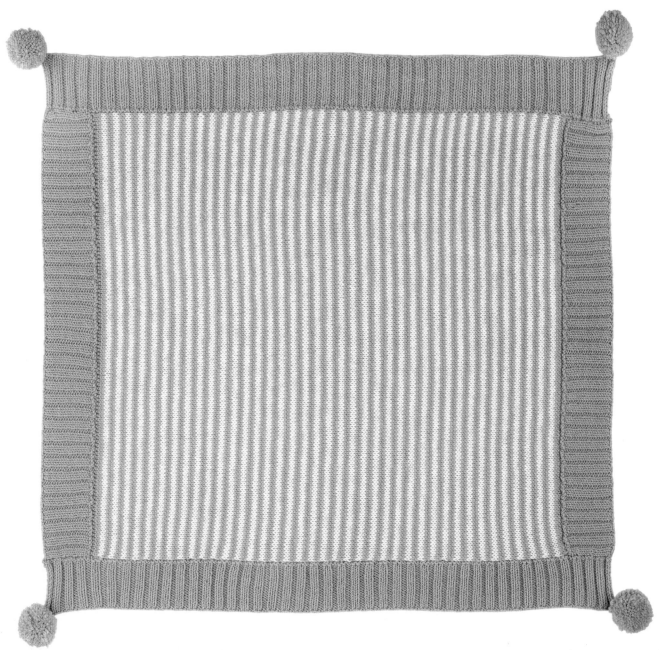

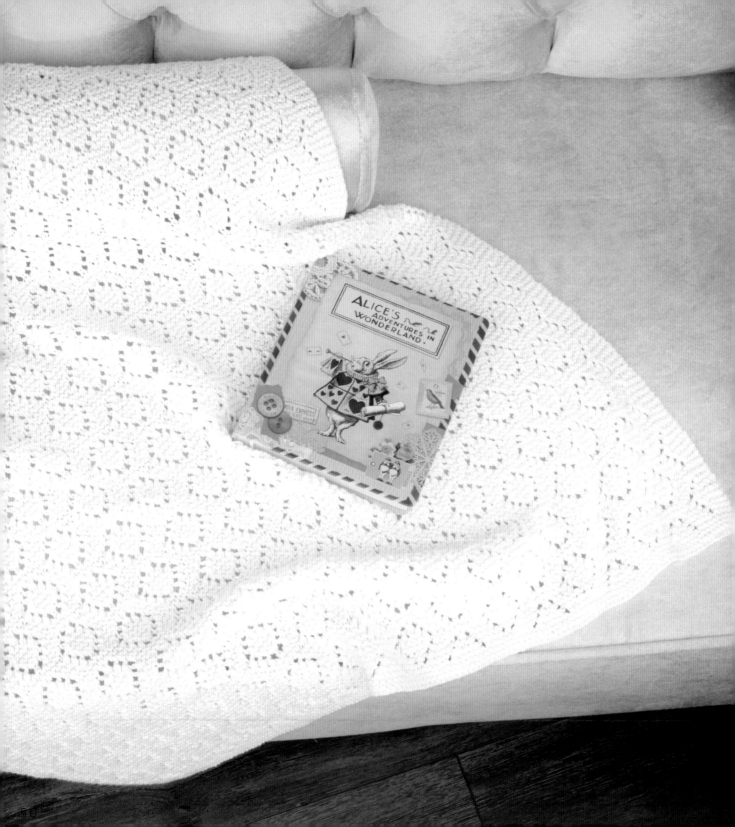

LACY DIAMONDS BLANKET

SIZE

Width (approx): 23½ [26: 28½] in (60 [66: 72] cm)
Length (approx): 31½ [34½: 37½] in (80 [87.5: 95] cm)

ABBREVIATIONS

See inside front flap

MATERIALS NEEDED

• **DMC Natura Just Cotton** (170 yd/155 m per 50g ball)
5 [6: 7] x balls of Ibiza (01)
• US 3 (3.25 mm) needles

GAUGE (TENSION)

25 sts and 44 rows to 4 in (10 cm) measured over patt using US 3 (3.25 mm) needles.

BLANKET

Using US 3 (3.25 mm) needles CO 151 [167: 183] sts.
Work in g st for 6 rows, ending with RS facing for next row.

Row 1 (RS): K4, *K4, yo, skpo, K3, K2tog, yo, K5, rep from * to last 3 sts, K3.

Row 2 and every foll alt row: Knit.

Row 3: K4, *yo, skpo, K3, yo, skpo, K1, K2tog, yo, K3, K2tog, yo, K1, rep from * to last 3 sts, K3.

Row 5: K4, *K1, yo, skpo, K3, yo, sl 1, K2tog, psso, yo, K3, K2tog, yo, K2, rep from * to last 3 sts, K3.

Row 7: K4, *K2, yo, skpo, K7, K2tog, yo, K3, rep from * to last 3 sts, K3.

Row 9: K4, *K1, K2tog, yo, K9, yo, skpo, K2, rep from * to last 3 sts, K3.

Row 11: K4, *K2tog, yo, K3, K2tog, yo, K1, yo, skpo, K3, yo, skpo, K1, rep from * to last 3 sts, K3.

Row 13: K3, K2tog, *yo, K3, K2tog, yo, K3, yo, skpo, K3, yo, sl 1, K2tog, psso, rep from * to last 5 sts, yo, skpo, K3.

Row 15: K4, *K3, K2tog, yo, K5, yo, skpo, K4, rep from * to last 3 sts, K3.

Row 16: Knit.
These 16 rows form patt.
Rep the last 16 rows 20 [22: 24] times more, ending with RS facing for next row. (Blanket should meas approx 30¾ [33½: 36½] in (78 [85.5: 93] cm.)
Work in g st for 6 rows, ending with RS facing for next row.
BO.

FINISHING

Block to measurements carefully following instructions on ball band

TWISTED LEAVES BLANKET

SIZE
Width (approx): 21½ [27½: 33½] in (55 [70: 85] cm)
Length (approx): 27½ [33½: 39½] in (70 [85: 100] cm)

ABBREVIATIONS
See inside front flap

SPECIAL ABBREVIATIONS
T2BP slip next st onto CN and leave at back of work, K1 tbl then P1 from CN

T2FP slip next st onto CN and leave at front of work, P1 then K1 tbl from CN

T3F slip next st onto CN and leave at front of work, K1 tbl, P1 then K1 tbl from CN

T3BP slip next st onto CN and leave at back of work, (K1 tbl) twice then P1 from CN

T3FP slip next 2 sts onto CN and leave at front of work, P1 then (K1 tbl) twice from CN

MB knit into front and back then front again of next st, turn, P3, turn, K3, turn, P1, P2tog, turn, K2tog.

MATERIALS NEEDED
• **DMC Woolly** (136 yd/125 m per 50g ball)
6 [9: 11] x balls of White (001)
• US 6 (4 mm) needles

GAUGE (TENSION)
28 sts and 35 rows to 4 in (10 cm) measured over patt using US 6 (4 mm) needles.

BLANKET

Using US 6 (4 mm) needles CO 153 [195: 237] sts.
Place charts

Next row (RS): K5, work next 17 sts as row 1 of chart A, *work next 25 sts as row 1 of chart B, work next 17 sts as row 1 of chart A, rep from * to last 5 sts, K5.
Next row: K5, work next 17 sts as row 2 of chart A, *work next 25 sts as row 2 of chart B, work next 17 sts as row 2 of chart A, rep from * to last 5 sts, K5.
These 2 rows set the sts - central 143 [185: 227] sts in patt from charts with 5 edge sts either side in g st for border.
Cont as set until work meas 27½ [33½: 39½] in (70 [85: 100] cm), ending with RS facing for next row.
BO in patt.

FINISHING

Block to measurements carefully following instructions on ball band.

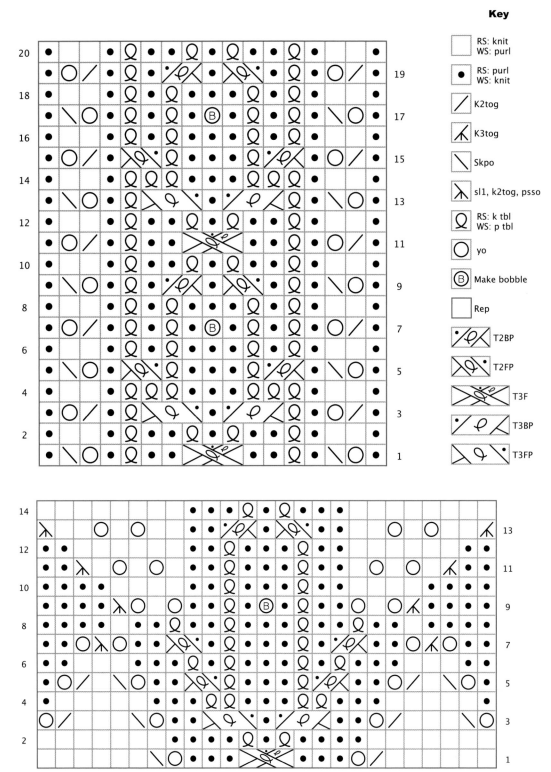

Chart A

Key

▢	RS: knit / WS: purl
•	RS: purl / WS: knit
╱	K2tog
⋏	K3tog
╲	Skpo
⅄	sl1, k2tog, psso
Ϙ	RS: k tbl / WS: p tbl
◯	yo
Ⓑ	Make bobble
▢	Rep
⋅Ϙ╱	T2BP
╲Ϙ⋅	T2FP
⋋Ϙ⋅	T3F
⋅Ϙ╲	T3BP
╱Ϙ⋅	T3FP

TEXTURED BLANKET

SIZE
Width (approx): 21½ [26½: 31½] in (55 [67.5: 80] cm)
Length (approx): 25½ [31½: 35½] in (65 [80: 90] cm)

ABBREVIATIONS
See inside front flap

SPECIAL ABBREVIATIONS
C6B slip next 3 sts onto CN and leave at front of work, K3, then K3 from CN

MATERIALS NEEDED
• **DMC Woolly** (136 yd/125 m per 50g ball)
5 [7: 9] x balls of Teal (077)
• US 5 (3.75 mm) needles
• US 6 (4 mm) needles
• Cable needle

GAUGE (TENSION)
27 sts and 32 rows to 4 in (10 cm) measured over patt using US 6 (4 mm) needles.

BLANKET

Using US 5 (3.75 mm) needles CO 129 [159: 189] sts. Work in g st for 12 [14: 16] rows, ending with RS facing for next row.

Next row (RS): K7 [8: 9], (Kfb) 3 times, *K25, (Kfb) 3 times, rep from * to last 7 [8: 9] sts, K7 [8: 9]. 144 [177: 210] sts. Change to US 6 (4 mm) needles.

Next row (WS): K7 [8: 9], P6, *K2, P21, K2, P6, rep from * to last 7 [8: 9] sts, K7 [8: 9]. 144 [177: 210] sts.

Row 1 (RS): K5 [6: 7], P2, K6, P2, *K1, P1, (K5, P1) 3 times, K1, P2, K6, P2 rep from * to last 5 [6: 7] sts, K5 [6: 7].

Row 2: K7 [8: 9], P6, *K2, P2, K1, (P3, K1, P1, K1) twice, P3, K1,
P2, K2, P6, rep from * to last 7 [8: 9] sts, K7 [8: 9].

Row 3: K5 [6: 7], P2, C6B, P2, *(K3, P1, K1, P1) 3 times, K3, P2, C6B, P2, rep from * to last 5 [6: 7] sts, K5 [6: 7].

Row 4: K7 [8: 9], P6, *K2, P4, K1, (P5, K1) twice, P4, K2, P6, rep from * to last 7 [8: 9] sts, K7 [8: 9].

Row 5: K5 [6: 7], P2, K6, P2, *(K3, P1, K1, P1) 3 times, K3, P2, K6, P2, rep from * to last 5 [6: 7] sts, K5 [6: 7].

Row 6: As row 2.

These 6 rows form patt.

Cont in patt until work meas approx 24¼ [30: 33½] in (61.5 [76: 85] cm), ending with row 4 of patt and RS facing for next row. Change to US 5 (3.75 mm) needles.

Next row (RS): K7 [8: 9], (K2tog) 3 times, *K25, (K2tog) 3 times, rep from * to last 7 [8: 9] sts, K7 [8: 9]. 129 [159: 189] sts.

Work in g st for 11 [13: 15] rows, ending with RS facing for next row.
BO.

FINISHING

Block to measurements carefully following instructions on ball band.

LITTLE KISSES BLANKET

SIZE

Width (approx): 23¾ [28: 32¼] in (60.5 [71.5: 82] cm)
Length (approx): 27½ [32¼: 36½] in (70 [82: 93] cm)

ABBREVIATIONS

See inside front flap

SPECIAL ABBREVIATIONS

C4F slip next 2 sts onto CN and leave at front of work, K2, then K2 from CN

C4BP slip next 2 sts onto CN and leave at back of work, K2, then P2 from CN

C4FP slip next 2 sts onto CN and leave at front of work, P2, then K2 from CN

MATERIALS NEEDED

• **DMC Woolly** (136 yd/125 m per 50g ball)
5 [6: 8] x balls of Teal (077)
• US 5 (3.75 mm) needles
• US 6 (4 mm) needles
• Cable needle

GAUGE (TENSION)

25 sts and 29 rows to 4 in (10 cm) measured over patt using US 6 (4 mm) needles.

BLANKET

Using US 5 (3.75 mm) needles CO 131 [155: 179] sts.
Work in g st for 19 [21: 23] rows, ending with WS facing for next row.

Next row (WS): K11 [12: 13], *K2, Kfb, K5, Kfb, K2, rep from * to last 10 [11: 12] sts, K10 [11: 12]. 151 [179: 207] sts.
Change to US 6 (4 mm) needles.
Place chart

Next row (RS): K10 [11: 12], work next 131 [157: 183] sts as row 1 of chart as folls, beg and ending rows as indicated and repeating the 26 st patt rep section in red 5 [6: 7] times across row, K10 [11: 12].
Last row set the sts - central 131 [157: 183] sts in patt from chart with 10 [11: 12] edge sts either side in g st for border. Keeping patt correct and starting with row 2 of chart, cont as set until all 28 rows of chart has been completed 7 [8: 9] times in total, ending with RS facing for next row. Change to US 5 (3.75 mm) needles.

Next row (RS): K10 [11: 12], *K2, K2tog, K5, K2tog, K2, rep from * to last 11 [12: 13] sts, K11 [12: 13]. 131 [155: 179] sts.
Work in g st for 19 [21: 23] rows, ending with RS facing for next row.
BO.

FINISHING

Block to measurements carefully following instructions on ball band.

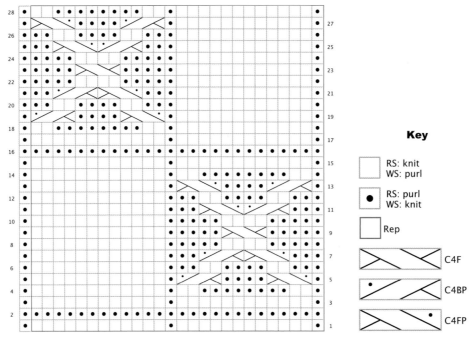

Key

▢	RS: knit WS: purl
●	RS: purl WS: knit
▢	Rep
✕✕	C4F
·╱╲	C4BP
╲╱·	C4FP

LACE AND CABLE BLANKET

SIZE

Width (approx): 24 [26: 28] in (61 [66: 71] cm)
Length (approx): 27½ [30: 32¼] in (70 [76: 82] cm)

ABBREVIATIONS

See inside front flap

SPECIAL ABBREVIATION

C5F slip next 2 sts onto CN and leave at front of work, K3, then K2 from CN

MATERIALS NEEDED

• **DMC Natura Just Cotton** (170 yd/155 m per 50g ball)
5 [6: 7] x balls of Rose Layette (06)
• US 3 (3.25 mm) needles
• Cable needle

GAUGE (TENSION)

28 sts and 38 rows to 4 in (10 cm) measured over main patt using US 3 (3.25 mm) needles.

BLANKET

Using US 3 (3.25 mm) needles CO 167 [181: 195] sts.

BOTTOM BORDER

Rows 1 and 2: Knit.

Row 3: K1, *yo, K2tog, rep from * to end.

Row 4: Knit.
These 4 rows form bottom border patt.
Cont in bottom border patt for a further 14 rows, ending with RS facing for next row.

MAIN PATT

Row 1 (RS): K1, (yo, K2tog) 4 times, P2, *K5, P2, rep from * to last 9 sts, (K2tog, yo) 4 times, K1.

Rows 2 and 4: K11, P5, *K2, P5, rep from * to last 11 sts, K11.

Row 3: K9, *P2, K5, rep from * to last 11 sts, P2, K9.

Rows 5 to 8: As rows 1 to 4.

Row 9: K1, (yo, K2tog) 4 times, P2, *C5F, P2, rep from * to last 9 sts, (K2tog, yo) 4 times, K1.

Rows 10 to 16: As rows 2 to 8.

Row 17: As row 1.

Row 18: Knit.

Row 19: As row 3.

Row 20: As row 18.

Row 21: K1, (yo, K2tog) 4 times, P2, *K1, (yo, K2tog) twice, P2, rep from * to last 9 sts, (K2tog, yo) 4 times, K1.

Rows 22 to 24: As rows 18 to 20.
Rep the last 24 rows 7 [8: 9] times more then rows 1 to 18 once more, ending with RS facing for next row.

TOP BORDER

Rows 1 and 2: Knit.

Row 3: K1, *yo, K2tog, rep from * to end.

Row 4: Knit.
These 4 rows form top border patt.
Cont in top border patt for a further 14 rows, ending with RS facing for next row.
BO knitwise.

FINISHING

Block to measurements carefully following instructions on ball band.

CABLE AND RIDGE STITCH BLANKET

SIZE

Width (approx): 24 [26¼: 28¼] in (61 [66.5: 72] cm)
Length (approx): 29 [31¼: 33½] in (74 [79.5: 85] cm)

ABBREVIATIONS

See inside front flap

SPECIAL ABBREVIATION

C6F slip next 3 sts onto CN and leave at front of work, K3, then K3 from CN

MATERIALS NEEDED

• **DMC Woolly** (136 yd/125 m per 50g ball)
6 [8: 10] x balls of Light Blue (071)
• US 5 (3.75 mm) needles
• US 6 (4 mm) needles
• Cable needle

GAUGE (TENSION)

27 sts and 32 rows to 4 in (10 cm) measured over patt using US 6 (4 mm) needles.

BLANKET

Using US 5 (3.75 mm) needles CO 145 [158: 171] sts.
Work in g st for 15 rows, ending with **WS** facing for next row.

Next row (WS): K13, (Kfb) twice, K3, *K8, (Kfb) twice, K3, rep from * to last 10 sts, K10. 165 [180: 195] sts.
Change to US 6 (4 mm) needles.

Row 1 (RS): K10, P2, K6, P2, *K5, P2, K6, P2, rep from * to last 10 sts, K10.

Row 2: K12, P6, *K2, P5, K2, P6, rep from * to last 12 sts, K12.

Row 3: As row 1.

Row 4: K12, P6, *K9, P6, rep from * to last 12 sts, K12.

Row 5: K10, P2, C6F, *P9, C6F, rep from * to last 12 sts, P2, K10.

Row 6: As row 4.
These 6 rows form patt.
Cont in patt until work meas approx 27½ [29¾: 31¾] in (70 [75.5: 81] cm), ending with row 2 and RS facing for next row.
Change to US 5 (3.75 mm) needles.

Next row (RS): K13, (K2tog) twice, K3, *K8, (K2tog) twice, K3, rep from * to last 10 sts, K10. 145 [158: 171] sts.
Work in g st for 15 rows, ending with RS facing for next row.
BO knitwise.

FINISHING

Block to measurements carefully following instructions on ball band.

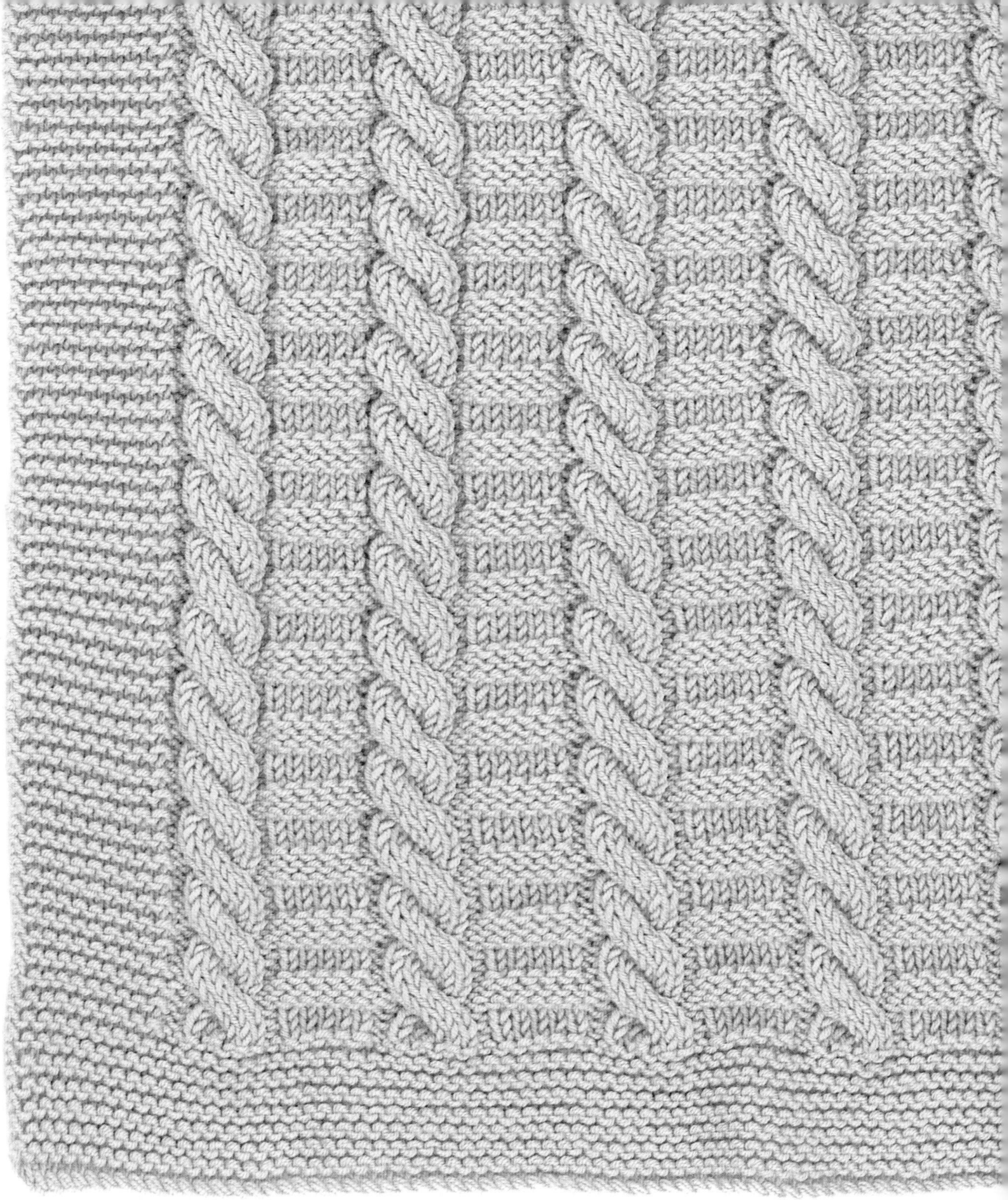

SEED MOSS STITCH AND LACE BLANKET

SIZE
Width (approx): 23½ [28¼: 33] in (60 [72: 84] cm)
Length (approx): 32½ [36½: 41] in (83 [93: 104] cm)

ABBREVIATIONS
See inside front flap

MATERIALS NEEDED
• **DMC Woolly** (136 yd/125 m per 50g ball)
6 [8: 10] x balls of Peach (101)
• US 6 (4 mm) needles

GAUGE (TENSION)
23 sts and 36 rows to 4 in (10 cm) measured over patt using US 6 (4 mm) needles.

BLANKET

Using US 6 (4 mm) needles CO 137 [165: 193] sts.

Row 1 (RS): K1, *P1, K1, rep from * to end.
Last row forms Seed (Moss) stitch.
Cont in Seed (Moss) stitch for a further 13 [15: 17] rows, ending with RS facing for next row.

PLACE CHART
12 st rep plus 1

Next row (RS): (K1, P1) 4 [5: 6] times, work next 121 [145: 169] sts as row 1 of chart, (P1, K1) 4 [5: 6] times.

Next row: (K1, P1) 4 [5: 6] times, work next 121 [145: 169] sts as row 2 of chart, (P1, K1) 4 [5: 6] times.
These 2 rows set the sts - central 121 [145: 169] sts in patt from chart with 8 [10: 12] edge sts either side in Seed (Moss) st for border.
Cont as set until all 30 rows of chart has been completed, ending with RS facing for next row.
Now rep the 30 rows as set 7 [8: 9] times more then rows 1 to 24, ending with RS facing for next row.

Row 1 (RS): K1, *P1, K1, rep from * to end. Last row forms Seed (Moss) stitch. Cont in Seed (Moss) stitch for a further 13 [15: 17] rows, ending with RS facing for next row.
BO.

FINISHING

Block to measurements carefully following instructions on ball band.

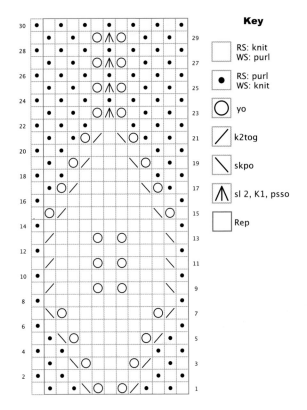

Key

☐	RS: knit WS: purl
●	RS: purl WS: knit
○	yo
╱	k2tog
╲	skpo
⋀	sl 2, K1, psso
☐	Rep

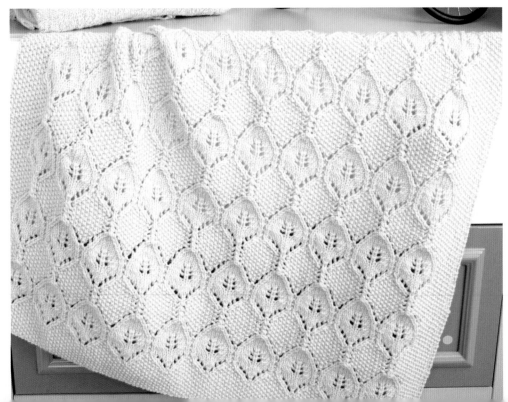

74

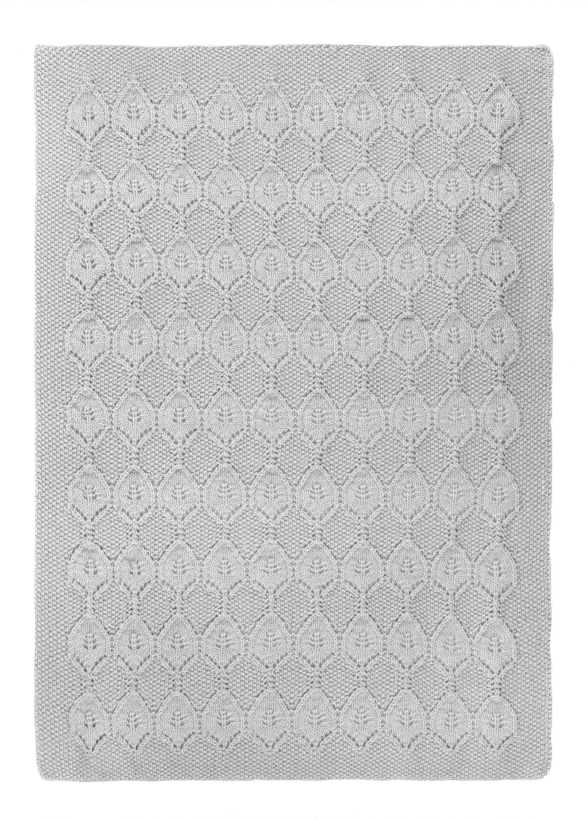

LACY ZIG ZAG BLANKET

SIZE
Width (approx): 23½ [27: 30¼] in (60 [68.5: 77] cm)
Length (approx): 28¾ [31¾: 34¾] in (73 [80.5: 88] cm)

ABBREVIATIONS
See inside front flap

MATERIALS NEEDED
• DMC Woolly (136 yd/125 m per 50g ball)
6 [8: 10] x balls of Pale Pink (041)
• US 6 (4 mm) needles

GAUGE (TENSION)
23 sts and 36 rows to 4 in (10 cm) measured over patt using US 6 (4 mm) needles.

BLANKET

Using US 6 (4 mm) needles CO 137 [157: 177] sts.

Next row (RS): K1, *P1, K1, rep from * to end.
Rep the last row 13 [15: 17] times more, ending with RS facing for next row.

Row 1 (RS): (K1, P1) 4 [5: 6] times, *K1, yo, skpo, K3, K2tog, yo, rep from * to last 9 [11: 13] sts, K1, (P1, K1) 4 [5: 6] times.

Rows 2, 4 and 6: (K1, P1) 4 [5: 6] times, P to last 8 [10: 12] sts, (P1, K1) 4 [5: 6] times.

Row 3: (K1, P1) 4 [5: 6] times, *K2, yo, skpo, K1, K2tog, yo, K1, rep from * to last 9 [11: 13] sts, K1, (P1, K1) 4 [5: 6] times.

Row 5: (K1, P1) 4 [5: 6] times, *K3, yo, sl 1, K2tog, psso, yo, K2, rep from * to last 9 [11: 13] sts, K1, (P1, K1) 4 [5: 6] times.

Rows 7 to 12: K1, *P1, K1, rep from * to end.
These 12 rows form patt.
Rep the last 12 rows 18 [20: 22] times more, then work rows 1 to 6 once more, ending with RS facing for next row.

Next row (RS): K1, *P1, K1, rep from * to end.
Rep the last row 13 [15: 17] times more, ending with RS facing for next row.
BO in patt.

FINISHING
Block to measurements carefully following instructions on ball band.

PATCHWORK BLANKET

SIZE

Width (approx): 19½ [24½: 29½] in (50 [62.5: 75] cm)
Length (approx): 19½ [24½: 29½] in (50 [62.5: 75] cm)

ABBREVIATIONS

See inside front flap

MATERIALS NEEDED

•**DMC Woolly** (136 yd/125 m per 50g ball)
1 [2: 2] x balls of Turquoise (074) **A**
1 [2: 2] x balls of Bright Pink (054) **B**
1 [2: 2] x balls of Yellow (093) **C**
1 [2: 2] x balls of Orange (102) **D**
1 [2: 2] x balls of Green (081) **E**
1 [1: 1] x balls of Purple (065) **F**
• US 6 (4 mm) needles

GAUGE (TENSION)

24 sts and 40 rows to 4 in (10 cm) measured over seed (moss) st using US 6 (4 mm) needles.

SEED (MOSS) ST

Row 1: K1, *P1, K1, rep from * to end.
Rep last row throughout.

BLANKET

NOTE: Blanket is worked in 5 strips then joined together.

STRIP ONE

Using US 6 (4 mm) needles and yarn **A** CO 25 [31: 37] sts. Work in seed (moss) st for 41 [51: 61] rows, ending with **WS** facing for next row. Change to yarn **B**.

Next row (WS): Purl.
Work in seed (moss) st for 41 [51: 61] rows, ending with **WS** facing for next row. Change to yarn **C**.

Next row (WS): Purl.
Work in seed (moss) st for 41 [51: 61] rows, ending with **WS** facing for next row. Change to yarn **D**.

Next row (WS): Purl.
Work in seed (moss) st for 41 [51: 61] rows, ending with **WS** facing for next row. Change to yarn **E**.

Next row (WS): Purl.
Work in seed (moss) st for 41 [51: 61] rows, ending with **WS** facing for next row. Using yarn **E** BO in patt for top edge.

STRIP TWO

Using US 6 (4 mm) needles and yarn **D** CO 25 [31: 37] sts. Work in seed (moss) st for 41 [51: 61] rows, ending with **WS** facing for next row. Change to yarn **A**.

Next row (WS): Purl.
Work in seed (moss) st for 41 [51: 61] rows, ending with **WS** facing for next row. Change to yarn **B**.

Next row (WS): Purl.
Work in seed (moss) st for 41 [51: 61] rows, ending with **WS** facing for next row. Change to yarn **C**.

Next row (WS): Purl.
Work in seed (moss) st for 41 [51: 61] rows, ending with **WS** facing for next row. Change to yarn **D**.
Next row (WS): Purl.
Work in seed (moss) st for 41 [51: 61] rows, ending with **WS** facing for next row. Using yarn **D** BO in patt for top edge.

STRIP THREE

Using US 6 (4 mm) needles and yarn **E** CO 25 [31: 37] sts. Work in seed (moss) st for 41 [51: 61] rows, ending with **WS** facing for next row. Change to yarn **D**.

Next row (WS): Purl.
Work in seed (moss) st for 41 [51: 61] rows, ending with **WS** facing for next row. Change to yarn **A**.

Next row (WS): Purl.
Work in seed (moss) st for 41 [51: 61] rows, ending with **WS** facing for next row. Change to yarn **B**.

Next row (WS): Purl.
Work in seed (moss) st for 41 [51: 61] rows, ending with **WS** facing for next row. Change to yarn **C**.

Next row (WS): Purl.
Work in seed (moss) st for 41 [51: 61] rows, ending with **WS** facing for next row. Using yarn **C** BO in patt for top edge.

STRIP FOUR

Using US 6 (4 mm) needles and yarn **C** CO 25 [31: 37] sts. Work in seed (moss) st for 41 [51: 61] rows, ending with **WS** facing for next row. Change to yarn **E**.

Next row (WS): Purl.
Work in seed (moss) st for 41 [51: 61] rows, ending with **WS** facing for next row. Change to yarn **D**.

Next row (WS): Purl.
Work in seed (moss) st for 41 [51: 61] rows, ending with **WS** facing for next row. Change to yarn **A**.

Next row (WS): Purl.
Work in seed (moss) st for 41 [51: 61] rows, ending with **WS** facing for next row. Change to yarn **B**.

Next row (WS): Purl.
Work in seed (moss) st for 41 [51: 61] rows, ending with **WS** facing for next row. Using yarn **B** BO in patt for top edge.

STRIP FIVE

Using US 6 (4 mm) needles and yarn **B** CO 25 [31: 37] sts. Work in seed (moss) st for 41 [51: 61] rows, ending with **WS** facing for next row. Change to yarn **C**.

Next row (WS): Purl.
Work in seed (moss) st for 41 [51: 61] rows, ending with **WS** facing for next row. Change to yarn **E**.

Next row (WS): Purl.
Work in seed (moss) st for 41 [51: 61] rows, ending with **WS** facing for next row. Change to yarn **D**.

Next row (WS): Purl.
Work in seed (moss) st for 41 [51: 61] rows, ending with **WS** facing for next row. Change to yarn **A**.
Next row (WS): Purl.
Work in seed (moss) st for 41 [51: 61] rows, ending with **WS** facing for next row.
Using yarn **A** BO in patt for top edge.

FINISHING

Weave in loose ends. Making sure all CO edges are at the bottom edge of the blanket, seam the 5 strips together (see diagram below) using backstitch or mattress stitch if preferred. Block to measurements. Using yarn **F** work blanket stitch evenly around the entire outer edge as shown in photograph.

ANCHOR BLANKET

SIZE
Width (approx): 23½ [28: 32½] in (60 [71: 82.5] cm)
Length (approx): 25¾ [29½: 34½] in (65.5 [75: 87.5] cm)

ABBREVIATIONS
See inside front flap

MATERIALS NEEDED
• **DMC Woolly** (136 yd/125 m per 50g ball)
2 [3: 3] x balls of Blue (075) **A**
2 [3: 3] x balls of Cream (003) **B**
3 [3: 3] x balls of Red (052) **C**
• US 3 (3.25 mm) needles
• US 6 (4 mm) needles

GAUGE (TENSION)
23 sts and 29 rows to 4 in (10 cm) measured over st st using US 5 (4 mm) needles.

BLANKET
Using US 6 (4 mm) needles and yarn **A** CO 117 [143: 169] sts.
Place chart. Using the intarsia method as described on (page 23), beg and ending rows as indicated on chart and beg with a K row, working entirely in st st repeating the 26 st rep section in red 2 [3: 4] times across each row, work rows 1 to 64, 2 [3: 3] times then rows 1 to 36, 1 [0: 1] times more, ending with RS facing for next row. BO using yarn **A**.

BOTTOM AND TOP BORDERS (both alike)
With RS facing, using US 3 (3.25mm) needles and yarn **C** pick up and Knit 140 [164: 188] sts evenly along CO or BO edge.

Next row (WS): Knit.

Row 1 (RS): K3, P2, *K2, P2, rep from * to last 3 sts, K3.

Row 2: K1, P2, *K2, P2, rep from * to last st, K1. These 2 rows form rib. Cont in rib for a further 16 rows, ending with RS facing for next row.
BO in rib.

SIDE BORDERS (both alike)
With RS facing, using US 3 (3.25 mm) needles and yarn **C** pick up and Knit 15 sts evenly along border, 154 [166: 178] sts evenly along side edge of blanket and 15 sts evenly along border. 184 [196: 208] sts.

Next row (WS): Knit.

Row 1 (RS): K3, P2, *K2, P2, rep from * to last 3 sts, K3.

Row 2: K1, P2, *K2, P2, rep from * to last st, K1.
These 2 rows form rib. Cont in rib for a further 16 rows, ending with RS facing for next row. BO in rib.

FINISHING
Block to measurements carefully following instructions on ball band.

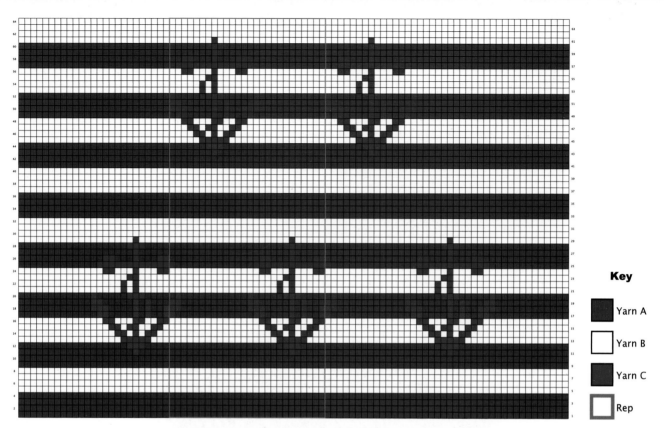

Key

■	Yarn A
□	Yarn B
■	Yarn C
▢	Rep

SAILBOAT BLANKET

SIZE
Width (approx): 24½ in (62.5 cm)
Length (approx): 34½ in (88 cm)

ABBREVIATIONS
See inside front flap

SPECIAL ABBREVIATION
C8B slip next 4 sts onto CN and leave at back of work, K4, then K4 from CN

MATERIALS NEEDED
• **DMC Natura Just Cotton** (170 yd/155 m per 50g ball)
2 x balls of Star Light (27) **A**
2 x balls of Passion (23) **B**
4 x balls of Ivory (35) **C**
• US 3 (3.25 mm) needles

GAUGE (TENSION)
28 sts and 36 rows to 4 in (10 cm) measured over st st using US 3 (3.25 mm) needles.

STRIPE SEQUENCE

Rows 1 to 4: Using yarn **B.**

Rows 5 to 8: Using yarn **C.**
These 8 rows form stripe patt and are repeated.

BLANKET

STRIP ONE

Using US 3 (3.25 mm) needles and yarn **A** CO 55 sts.

Rows 1 to 60: Using the intarsia method as described on (page 23), beg and ending rows as indicated on chart and beg with a K row, working entirely in st st until all 60 rows have been completed, ending with RS facing for next row.

Rows 61 to 120: Beg with a K row, work entirely in st st in stripe sequence (see left column), ending with row 4 of patt and RS facing for next row.

Rows 121 to 180: As rows 1 to 60.

Rows 181 to 240: As rows 61 to 120.

Rows 241 to 300: As rows 1 to 60.
BO knitwise using yarn **A.**

STRIP TWO

Using US 3 (3.25 mm) needles and yarn **B** CO 55 sts.

Rows 1 to 60: Beg with a K row, work entirely in st st in stripe sequence (see left column), ending with row 4 of patt and RS facing for next row.

Rows 61 to 120: Using the intarsia method as described on (page 23), beg and ending rows as indicated on chart and beg with a K row, working entirely in st st until all 60 rows have been completed, ending with RS facing for next row.

Rows 121 to 180: As rows 1 to 60.

Rows 181 to 240: As rows 61 to 120.

Rows 241 to 300: As rows 1 to 60.
BO knitwise using yarn **B.**

STRIP THREE

Work as given for strip one.

FINISHING

Weave in loose ends.
Sew the strips together noting that strip two is the centre
with strip one and three either side.
Block to measurements carefully following instructions
on ball band.

BORDER

Using US 3 (3.25 mm) needles and yarn **C** CO 10 sts.

Row 1 (RS): Knit.

Row 2: K2, P8.

Rows 3 to 6: As rows 1 and 2 twice.

Row 7 (RS): C8B, K2.

Row 8: As row 2.

Row 9: As row 1.

Row 10: As row 2.
These 10 rows form patt.
Cont in patt until straight edge of border fits around the
entire outer edge of the blanket, sewing in place as you go.
When border meets CO edge of border, ending with RS
facing, BO. Join CO and BO edges of border together.

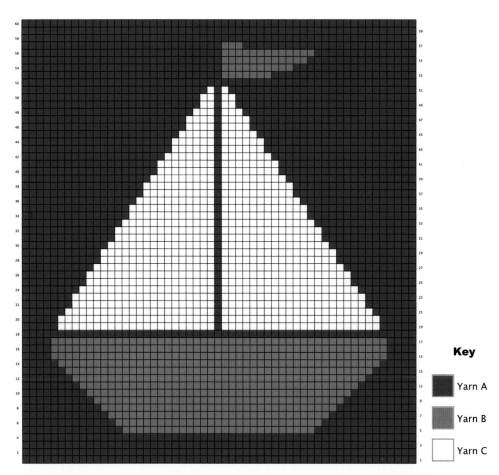

Key

Yarn A

Yarn B

Yarn C

FLOWER BLANKET

SIZE
Width (approx): 25 in (64 cm)
Length (approx): 34½ in (88 cm)

ABBREVIATIONS
See inside front flap

MATERIALS NEEDED
•**DMC Natura Just Cotton** (170 yd/155 m per 50g ball)
3 x balls of Rose Layette (06) **A**
4 x balls of Crimson (61) **B**
2 x balls of Erica (51) **C**
• US 3 (3.25 mm) needles

GAUGE (TENSION)
28 sts and 36 rows to 4 in (10 cm) measured over st st using US 3 (3.25 mm) needles.

STRIPE SEQUENCE
Rows 1 to 4: Using yarn **B.**
Rows 5 to 8: Using yarn **C.**
These 8 rows form stripe patt and are repeated.

BLANKET

STRIP ONE

Using US 3 (3.25 mm) needles and yarn **A** CO 56 sts.

Rows 1 to 60: Using the intarsia method as described on (page 23), beg and ending as indicated on chart, until all 60 rows have been completed, ending with RS facing for next row.

Rows 61 to 120: Beg with a K row, work entirely in st st in stripe sequence (see left column), ending with row 4 of patt and RS facing for next row.

Rows 121 to 180: As rows 1 to 60.

Rows 181 to 240: As rows 61 to 120.

Rows 241 to 300: As rows 1 to 60.
BO knitwise using yarn **A.**

STRIP TWO

Using US 3 (3.25 mm) needles and yarn **B** CO 56 sts.

Rows 1 to 60: Beg with a K row, work entirely in st st in stripe sequence (see left column, ending with row 4 of patt and RS facing for next row.

Rows 61 to 120: Using the intarsia method as described on (page 23), beg and ending as indicated on chart, until all 60 rows have been completed, ending with RS facing for next row.

Rows 121 to 180: As rows 1 to 60.

Rows 181 to 240: As rows 61 to 120.

Rows 241 to 300: As rows 1 to 60.
BO knitwise using yarn **B**.

STRIP THREE

Work as given for strip one.

FINISHING

Weave in loose ends.
Sew the strips together noting that strip two is the centre with strip one and three either side. Block to measurements carefully following instructions on ball band.

BORDER

Using US 3 (3.25 mm) needles and yarn CO 4 sts.

Row 1 (RS): K2, yo, K2. 5 sts.
Row 2 and every foll alt row: Knit.

Row 3: K3, yo, K2. 6 sts.

Row 5: K2, yo, K2tog, yo, K2. 7 sts.

Row 7: K3, yo, K2tog, yo, K2. 8 sts.

Row 8: BO 4 sts (1 st on right needle), K to end. 4 sts.
These 8 rows form patt.

Cont in patt until straight edge of border fits around the entire outer edge of the blanket, sewing in place as you go.
When border meets CO edge of border, ending with RS facing, BO. Join CO and BO edges of border together.

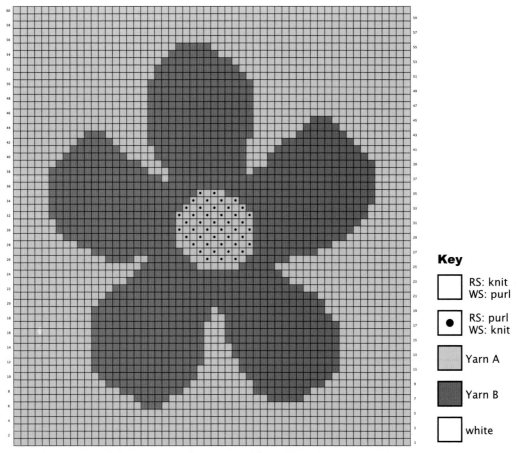

Key

☐	RS: knit WS: purl
⊡	RS: purl WS: knit
▦	Yarn A
■	Yarn B
☐	white

SHEEP BLANKET

SIZE
Width (approx): 24½ in (62.5 cm)
Length (approx): 34½ in (88 cm)

ABBREVIATIONS
See inside front flap

MATERIALS NEEDED
• **DMC Natura Just Cotton** (170 yd/155 m per 50g ball)
4 x balls of Pistache (13) **A**
2 x balls of Noir (11) **B**
2 x balls of Nacar (35) **C**
• US 3 (3.25 mm) needles

GAUGE (TENSION)
28 sts and 36 rows to 4 in (10 cm) measured over st st
using US 3 (3.25 mm) needles.

STRIPE SEQUENCE
Rows 1 to 4: Using yarn **B.**
Rows 5 to 8: Using yarn **A.**
These 8 rows form stripe patt and are repeated.

BLANKET

STRIP ONE
Using US 3 (3.25 mm) needles and yarn **A** CO 55 sts.

Rows 1 to 60: Using the intarsia method as described on
(page 23), beg and ending as indicated on chart,
until all 60 rows have been completed, ending with
RS facing for next row.

Rows 61 to 120: Beg with a K row, work entirely in st st in
stripe sequence (see left column), ending with row 4 of
patt and RS facing for next row.

Rows 121 to 180: As rows 1 to 60.

Rows 181 to 240: As rows 61 to 120.

Rows 241 to 300: As rows 1 to 60.
BO knitwise using yarn **A.**

STRIP TWO

Using US 3 (3.25 mm) needles and yarn **B** CO 55 sts.

Rows 1 to 60: Beg with a K row, work entirely in st st in
stripe sequence (see left column), ending with row 4 of
patt and RS facing for next row.

Rows 61 to 120: Using the intarsia method as described
on (page 23), beg and ending as indicated on chart, until
all 60 rows have been completed, ending with RS facing
for next row.

Rows 121 to 180: As rows 1 to 60.

Rows 181 to 240: As rows 61 to 120.

Rows 241 to 300: As rows 1 to 60.
BO knitwise using yarn **B**.

STRIP THREE

Work as given for strip one.

FINISHING

Weave in loose ends. Sew the strips together noting that strip two is the centre with strip one and three either side. Block to measurements carefully following instructions on ball band.

BORDER

Using US 3 (3.25 mm) needles and yarn **A** CO 5 sts.

Row 1 (RS): Sl 1, yo, K2tog, yo, K2. 6 sts.

Row 2 and every foll alt row: Knit.

Row 3: Sl 1, (yo, K2tog) twice, yo, K1. 7 sts.

Row 5: Sl 1, (yo, K2tog) twice, yo, K2. 8 sts.

Row 7: Sl 1, (yo, K2tog) 3 times, yo, K1. 9 sts.

Row 9: Sl 1, (yo, K2tog) 3 times, yo, K2. 10 sts.

Row 11: BO 6 sts (1 st on right needle), yo, K2tog, K1. 5 sts.

Row 12: Knit.

These 12 rows form patt.

Cont in patt until straight edge of border fits around the entire outer edge of the blanket, sewing in place as you go. When border meets CO edge of border, ending with RS facing, BO.

Join CO and BO edges of border together.

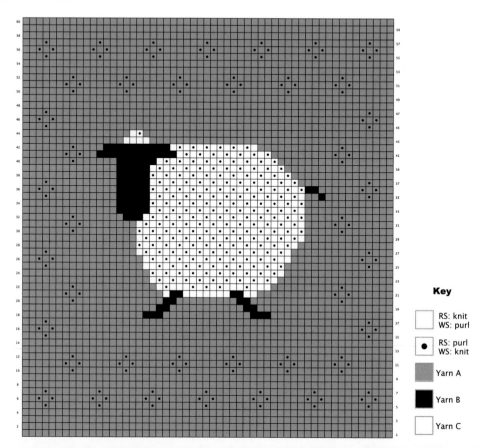

Key

□	RS: knit WS: purl
⊡	RS: purl WS: knit
▦	Yarn A
■	Yarn B
□	Yarn C

LACE AND BOBBLE BLANKET

SIZE
Width (approx): 27½ [30¾: 33¾] in (70 [78: 86] cm)
Length (approx): 30 [33: 36] in (76.5 [84: 91.5] cm)

ABBREVIATIONS
See inside front flap

SPECIAL ABBREVIATION
MB knit into front, back, then front again of next st, turn, P3, turn, K3, turn, P1, P2tog, turn, K2tog.

MATERIALS NEEDED
• **DMC Woolly** (136 yd/125 m per 50g ball)
5 [7: 9] x balls of Light Lime (092)
• US 6 (4 mm) needles

GAUGE (TENSION)
23 sts and 28 rows to 4 in (10 cm) measured over patt using US 6 (4 mm) needles.

BLANKET

Using US 6 (4 mm) needles CO 143 [161: 179] sts.

Row 1 (RS): Knit.

Row 2 and every foll alt row: Purl.

Row 3: K8, yo, skpo, *K16, yo, skpo, rep from * to last 7 sts, K7.

Row 5: K6, K2tog, yo, K1, yo, skpo, *K13, K2tog, yo, K1, yo, skpo, rep from * to last 6 sts, K6.

Row 7: K5, K2tog, yo, K3, yo, skpo, *K11, K2tog, yo, K3, yo, skpo, rep from * to last 5 sts, K5.

Row 9: K4, K2tog, yo, K2, MB, K2, yo, skpo, *K9, K2tog, yo, K2, MB, K2, yo, skpo, rep from * to last 4 sts, K4.

Row 11: Knit.

Row 13: K17, *yo, skpo, K16, rep from * to end.

Row 15: K15, K2tog, yo, K1, yo, skpo, *K13, K2tog, yo, K1, yo, skpo, rep from * to last 15 sts, K15.

Row 17: K14, K2tog, yo, K3, yo, skpo, *K11, K2tog, yo, K3, yo, skpo, rep from * to last 14 sts, K14.

Row 19: K13, K2tog, yo, K2, MB, K2, yo, skpo, *K9, K2tog, yo, K2, MB, K2, yo, skpo, rep from * to last 13 sts, K13.

Row 20: Purl.
These 20 rows form patt.
Rep last 20 rows 8 [9: 10] times more, then rows 1 to 12 once more, ending with RS facing for next row. BO.

FINISHING

Block to measurements carefully following instructions on ball band.

BORDER

Using US 6 (4 mm) needles CO 5 sts.

Row 1 (RS): K3, Kfb, K1. 6 sts.

Row 2 and every foll alt row: Knit.

Row 3: K4, Kfb, K1. 7 sts.

Row 5: K5, Kfb, K1. 8 sts.

Row 7: K6, Kfb, K1. 9 sts.

Row 9: K7, Kfb, K1. 10 sts.

Row 11: K8, Kfb, MB. 11 sts.

Row 12: BO 6 sts (1 st on right needle) K to end. 5 sts. These 12 rows form patt.

Cont in patt until straight edge of border fits along outer edge of blanket (sewing as you go), easing around corners and ending with row 11 and **WS** facing for next row.

BO knitwise (on **WS**).

Join remainder of border to blanket edge, then join CO and BO edges together.

SEED STITCH CHEVRON BLANKET

SIZE
Width (approx): 25 [29¼: 33½] in (63.75 [74.5: 85.5] cm)
Length (approx): 28¾ [33: 37] in (73 [83.5: 94] cm)

ABBREVIATIONS
See inside front flap

MATERIALS NEEDED
• **DMC Woolly** (136 yd/125 m per 50g ball)
7 [9: 11] x balls of Light Grey (121)
• US 5 (3.75 mm) needles

GAUGE (TENSION)
24 sts and 35 rows to 4 in (10 cm) measured over patt
using US 5 (3.75 mm) needles.

BLANKET

Using US 5 (3.75 mm) needles CO 153 [179: 205] sts.

Row 1 (RS): K1, *P1, K1, rep from * to end.
Last row forms patt.
Cont in patt for a further 15 [19: 23] rows, ending with RS
facing for next row.

Row 1 (RS): (K1, P1) 5 [6: 7] times, *K1, P3, K1, (P1, K1)
twice, P5, K1, (P1, K1) twice, P3, rep from * to last 11 [13:
15] sts, K1, (P1, K1) 5 [6: 7] times.

Row 2: (K1, P1) 5 [6: 7] times, P1, *P1, K3, P1, (K1, P1) twice,
K3, P1, (K1, P1) twice, K3, P2, rep from * to last 10 [12: 14]
sts, (P1, K1) 5 [6: 7] times.

Row 3: (K1, P1) 5 [6: 7] times, *K3, P3, K1, (P1, K1) 5 times,
P3, K2, rep from * to last 11 [13: 15] sts, K1, (P1, K1) 5 [6:
7] times.

Row 4: (K1, P1) 5 [6: 7] times, K1, *P3, K3, P1, (K1, P1) 4
times, K3, P3, K1, rep from * to last 10 [12: 14] sts, (P1, K1)
5 [6: 7] times.

Row 5: (K1, P1) 5 [6: 7] times, *P2, K3, P3, K1, (P1, K1) 3
times, P3, K3, P1, rep from * to last 11 [13: 15] sts, P1, (P1,
K1) 5 [6: 7] times.

Row 6: (K1, P1) 5 [6: 7] times, K1, *K2, P3, K3, P1, (K1, P1) twice, K3, P3, K3, rep from * to last 10 [12: 14] sts, (P1, K1) 5 [6: 7] times.

Row 7: (K1, P1) 5 [6: 7] times, *K1, P3, K3, P3, K1, P1, K1, P3, K3, P3, rep from * to last 11 [13: 15] sts, K1, (P1, K1) 5 [6: 7] times.

Row 8: (K1, P1) 5 [6: 7] times, K1, *P1, (K3, P3, K3, P1) twice, K1, rep from * to last 10 [12: 14] sts, (P1, K1) 5 [6: 7] times.

Row 9: (K1, P1) 5 [6: 7] times, *K1, P1, K1, P3, K3, P5, K3, P3, K1, P1, rep from * to last 11 [13: 15] sts, K1, (P1, K1) 5 [6: 7] times.

Row 10: (K1, P1) 5 [6: 7] times, K1, *P1, K1, P1, (K3, P3) twice, K3, (P1, K1) twice, rep from * to last 10 [12: 14] sts, (P1, K1) 5 [6: 7] times.

Row 11: (K1, P1) 5 [6: 7] times, *K1, (P1, K1) twice, P3, k3, P1, K3, P3, (K1, P1) twice, rep from * to last 11 [13: 15] sts, K1, (P1, K1) 5 [6: 7] times.

Row 12: (K1, P1) 5 [6: 7] times, K1, *P1, (K1, P1) twice, K3, P5, K3, (P1, K1) 3 times, rep from * to last 10 [12: 14] sts, (P1, K1) 5 [6: 7] times.

Row 13: (K1, P1) 5 [6: 7] times, *P2, K1, (P1, K1) twice, P3, K3, P3, (K1, P1) 3 times, rep from * to last 11 [13: 15] sts, P1, (P1, K1) 5 [6: 7] times.

Row 14: (K1, P1) 5 [6: 7] times, K1, *K2, P1, (K1, P1) twice, (K3, P1) twice, (K1, P1) twice, K3, rep from * to last 10 [12: 14] sts, (P1, K1) 5 [6: 7] times.

These 14 rows form patt.
Rep last 14 rows 15 [17: 19] times more, ending with RS facing for next row.

Next row (RS): K1, *P1, K1, rep from * to end.
Last row forms patt. Cont in patt for a further 15 [19: 23] rows, ending with RS facing for next row.
BO in patt.

FINISHING

Block to measurements carefully following instructions on ball band.

TWISTED TAILS BLANKET

SIZE

Width (approx): 27½ [31: 34½] in (70 [79: 88] cm)
Length (approx): 31½ [35½: 39½] in (80 [90: 100] cm)

ABBREVIATIONS

See inside front flap

MATERIALS NEEDED

• **DMC Woolly** (136 yd/125 m per 50g ball)
6 [8: 10] x balls of Light Pink (041)
• US 3 (3.25 mm) needles
• US 6 (4 mm) needles

GAUGE (TENSION)

25 sts and 28 rows to 4 in (10 cm) measured over patt
using US 6 (4 mm) needles.

BLANKET

Using US 6 (4 mm) needles CO 171 [195: 219] sts.

Row 1 (RS): K1, *P1, K1 tbl, yo, (K1 tbl, P1) twice, skpo, K1
tbl, (P1, K1 tbl) 4 times, K2tog, (P1, K1 tbl) twice, yo, K1 tbl,
rep from * to last 2 sts, P1, K1.

Row 2: K2, *P1 tbl, K1, yo, (P1 tbl, K1) twice, P2tog, K1, (P1
tbl, K1) 3 times, P2tog tbl, (K1, P1 tbl) twice, yo, K1, P1 tbl,
K1, rep from * to last st, K1.

Row 3: K1, *(P1, K1 tbl) twice, yo, (K1 tbl, P1) twice, skpo,
K1 tbl, (P1, K1 tbl) twice, K2tog, (P1, K1 tbl) twice, yo, K1 tbl,
P1, K1 tbl, rep from * to last 2 sts, P1, K1.

Row 4: K2, *(P1 tbl, K1) twice, yo, (P1 tbl, K1) twice, P2tog,
K1, P1 tbl, K1, P2tog tbl, (K1, P1 tbl) twice, yo, K1, (P1 tbl,
K1) twice, rep from * to last st, K1.

Row 5: K1, *(P1, K1 tbl) 3 times, yo, (K1 tbl, P1) twice,
skpo, K1 tbl, K2tog, (P1, K1 tbl) twice, yo, K1 tbl, (P1, K1
tbl) twice, rep from * to last 2 sts, P1, K1.

Row 6: K2, *yo, (P1 tbl, K1) 5 times, P3tog, (K1, P1 tbl) 5
times, yo, K1, rep from * to last st, K1.

Last 6 rows form patt.
Cont as set until work meas approx 30 [33½: 37½] in (76
[85.5: 95] cm), ending with a row 6 and RS facing for next row.

Change to US 3 (3.25 mm) needles.
Work in g st for 16 [18: 20] rows, ending with RS facing
for next row. BO.

FINISHING

Block to measurements carefully following instructions
on ball band.

BRODERIE ANGLAISE BLANKET

SIZE
Width (approx): 26¾ [30¾: 34¾] in (68 [78: 88] cm)
Length (approx): 26¾ [30¾: 34¾] in (68 [78: 88] cm)

ABBREVIATIONS
See inside front flap

MATERIALS NEEDED
DMC Woolly (136 yd/125 m per 50g ball)
5 [7: 9] x balls of Lilac (061)
US 5 (3.75 mm) needles

GAUGE (TENSION)
26 sts and 33 rows to 4 in (10 cm) measured over patt using US 5 (3.75 mm) needles.

BLANKET

Using US 5 (3.75 mm) needles CO 158 [184: 210] sts.

Next row (WS): Purl.

NOTE: This pattern has variable stitch counts and must only be counted after rows **4** and **8**.

Row 1 (RS): K1 [2: 3], *K4, K2tog, skpo, rep from * to last 5 [6: 7] sts, K5 [6: 7].

Row 2 and every foll alt row: K1, P to last st, K1.

Row 3: K1 [2: 3], *K4, K1 long right (insert the right needle 2 rows below into the space between the K2tog and the skpo, then knit a stitch, drawing up a loop onto the right needle), K2, K1 long left (insert the right needle into the same space as the K1 long right and knit a stitch, drawing up a loop onto the needle), rep from * to last 5 [6: 7] sts, K5 [6: 7].

Row 5: K1 [2: 3], *K2tog, skpo, K4, rep from * to last 5 [6: 7] sts, K2tog, skpo, K1 [2: 3].

Row 7: K1 [2: 3], *K1 long right, K2, K1 long left, K4, rep from * to last 3 [4: 5] sts, K1 long right, K2, K1 long left, K1 [2: 3].

Row 8: As row 2.

These 8 rows form patt.

Rep these last 8 rows 24 [28: 32] times more work should

measures approx 23½ [27¼: 31½] in (60 [70: 80] cm), ending with row 8 of patt and RS facing for next row. BO.

FINISHING

Block to measurements carefully following instructions on ball band.

BORDER

Using US 5 (3.75 mm) needles CO 4 sts.

Row 1 (RS): K2, yo, K2. 5 sts.

Row 2 and every foll alt row: Knit.

Row 3: K3, yo, K2. 6 sts.

Row 5: K2, yo, K2tog, yo, K2. 7 sts.

Row 7: K3, yo, K2tog, yo, K2. 8 sts.

Row 8: BO 4 sts (1 st on right needle) K to end. 4 sts. These 8 rows form patt.

Cont in patt until straight edge of border fits along outer edge of blanket (sewing as you go), easing around corners and ending with row 7 and **WS** facing for next row.

BO knitwise (on **WS**).

FINISHING

Join remainder of border to blanket edge, then join CO and BO edges together.

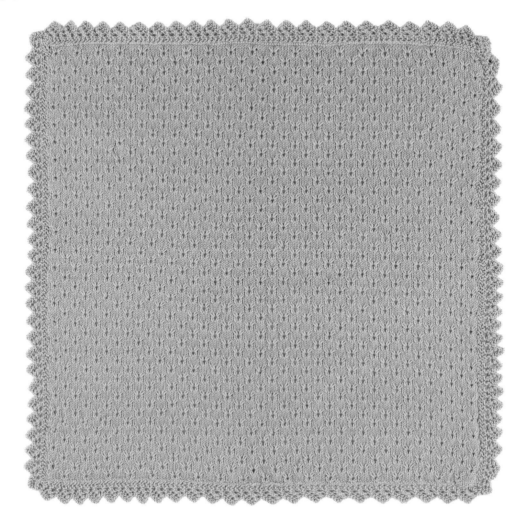

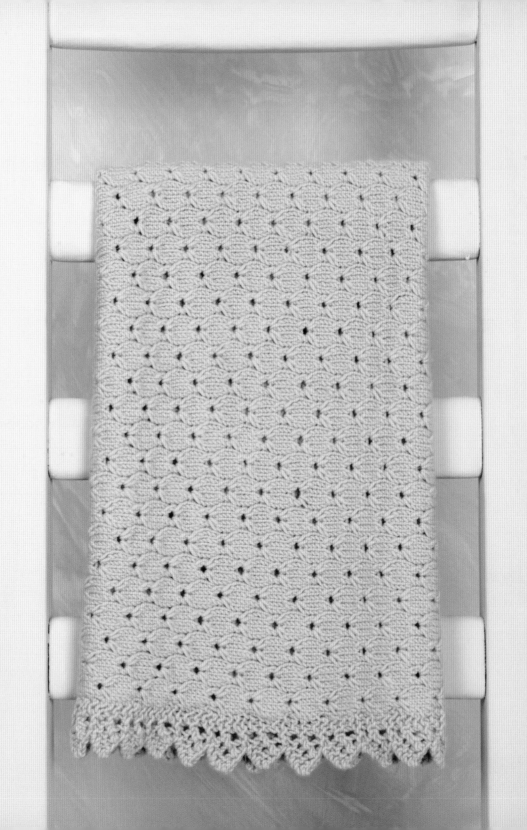

BOBBLE FLOWER AND LACE BLANKET

SIZE
Width (approx): 25½ in (65 cm)
Length (approx): 33½ in (85 cm)

ABBREVIATIONS
See inside front flap

SPECIAL ABBREVIATION
MB make bobble by knitting into front, back and front again of next st, turn, P3, turn, K3, turn, P3, turn, sl 1, K2tog, psso.

MATERIALS NEEDED
• **DMC Woolly** (136 yd/125 m per 50g ball)
7 x balls of Lilac (061)
• US 6 (4 mm) needles

GAUGE (TENSION)
23 sts and 32 rows to 4 in (10 cm) measured over st st using US 6 (4 mm) needles.

BLANKET

Using US 6 (4 mm) needles CO 153 sts.

Row 1 (RS): K1, *P1, K1, rep from * to end.
Rep last row 3 times more, ending with RS facing for next row.

BOTTOM BORDER

Row 1 (RS): K1, P1, K1, P to last 3 sts, K1, P1, K1.

Row 2: K1, P1, K to last 2 sts, P1, K1.

PLACE CHART

Row 1 (RS): K1, P1, K1, P3, *work next 15 sts as row 1 of chart, P3, rep from * to last 3 sts, K1, P1, K1.

Row 2: K1, P1, K4, *work next 15 sts as row 2 of chart, K3, rep from * to last 3 sts, K1, P1, K1.
These last 2 rows place chart with 3 sts of seed (moss) stitch either end with 3 sts in rev st st between the charts. Cont as set until all 32 rows of chart have been completed, ending with RS facing for next row.

MAIN SECTION

Row 1 (RS): K1, P1, K1, P3, work next 15 sts as row 1 of chart, P3, K105 sts, P3, work next 15 sts as row 1 of chart, P3, K1, P1, K1.

Row 2: K1, P1, K4, work next 15 sts as row 2 of chart, K3, P105, K3, work next 15 sts as row 2 of chart, K4, P1, K1.

Row 3: K1, P1, K1, P3, work next 15 sts as row 3 of chart, P3, K5, *skpo, yo, K1, yo, K2tog, K5, rep from * 9 times more, P3, work next 15 sts as row 3 of chart, P3, K1, P1, K1.

Row 4: K1, P1, K4, work next 15 sts as row 4 of chart, K3, P105, K3, work next 15 sts as row 4 of chart, K4, P1, K1.

Row 5: K1, P1, K1, P3, work next 15 sts as row 5 of chart, P3, K4, *skpo, yo, K1, (yo) twice, K2tog, yo, K2tog, K3, rep from * 9 times more, K1, P3, work next 15 sts as row 5 of chart, P3, K1, P1, K1.

Row 6: K1, P1, K4, work next 15 sts as row 6 of chart, K3, P105 dropping one strand of each double yo on previous row, K3, work next 15 sts as row 6 of chart, K4, P1, K1.

Row 7: K1, P1, K1, P3, work next 15 sts as row 7 of chart, P3, K5, *skpo, yo, K1, yo, K2tog, K5, rep from * 9 times more, P3, work next 15 sts as row 7 of chart, P3, K1, P1, K1.

Row 8: K1, P1, K4, work next 15 sts as row 8 of chart, K3, P105, K3, work next 15 sts as row 8 of chart, K4, P1, K1.

Row 9: K1, P1, K1, P3, work next 15 sts as row 9 of chart, P3, K105 sts, P3, work next 15 sts as row 9 of chart, P3, K1, P1, K1.

Row 10: K1, P1, K4, work next 15 sts as row 10 of chart, K3, P105, K3, work next 15 sts as row 10 of chart, K4, P1, K1.

Row 11: K1, P1, K1, P3, work next 15 sts as row 11 of chart, P3, K3, yo, K2tog, *K5, skpo, yo, K1, yo, K2tog, rep from * 8 times more, K5, skpo, yo, K3, P3, work next 15 sts as row 11 of chart, P3, K1, P1, K1.

Row 12: K1, P1, K4, work next 15 sts as row 12 of chart, K3, P105, K3, work next 15 sts as row 12 of chart, K4, P1, K1.

Row 13: K1, P1, K1, P3, work next 15 sts as row 13 of chart, P3, K2, (yo) twice, K2tog, yo, K2tog, *K3, skpo, yo, K1, (yo) twice, K2tog, yo, K2tog, rep from * 8 times more, K3, skpo, yo, K1, (yo) twice, K2tog, K1, P3, work next 15 sts as row 13 of chart, P3, K1, P1, K1.

Row 14: K1, P1, K4, work next 15 sts as row 14 of chart, K3, P105 dropping one strand of each double yo on previous row, K3, work next 15 sts as row 14 of chart, K4, P1, K1.

Row 15: K1, P1, K1, P3, work next 15 sts as row 15 of chart, P3, K3, yo, K2tog, *K5, skpo, yo, K1, yo, K2tog, rep from * 8 times more, K5, skpo, yo, K3, P3, work next 15 sts as row 15 of chart, P3, K1, P1, K1.

Row 16: K1, P1, K4, work next 15 sts as row 16 of chart, K3, P105, K3, work next 15 sts as row 16 of chart, K4, P1, K1.

Row 17: K1, P1, K1, P3, work next 15 sts as row 17 of chart, P3, K105 sts, P3, work next 15 sts as row 17 of chart, P3, K1, P1, K1.

Row 18: K1, P1, K4, work next 15 sts as row 18 of chart, K3, P105, K3, work next 15 sts as row 18 of chart, K4, P1, K1.

Row 19: K1, P1, K1, P3, work next 15 sts as row 19 of chart, P3, K5, *skpo, yo, K1, yo, K2tog, K5, rep from * 9 times more, P3, work next 15 sts as row 19 of chart, P3, K1, P1, K1.

Row 20: K1, P1, K4, work next 15 sts as row 20 of chart, K3, P105, K3, work next 15 sts as row 20 of chart, K4, P1, K1.

Row 21: K1, P1, K1, P3, work next 15 sts as row 21 of chart, P3, K4, *skpo, yo, K1, (yo) twice, K2tog, yo, K2tog, K3, rep from * 9 times more, K1, P3, work next 15 sts as row 21 of chart, P3, K1, P1, K1.

Row 22: K1, P1, K4, work next 15 sts as row 22 of chart, K3, P105 dropping one strand of each double yo on previous row, K3, work next 15 sts as row 22 of chart, K4, P1, K1.

Row 23: K1, P1, K1, P3, work next 15 sts as row 23 of chart, P3, K5, *skpo, yo, K1, yo, K2tog, K5, rep from * 9 times more, P3, work next 15 sts as row 23 of chart, P3, K1, P1, K1.

Row 24: K1, P1, K4, work next 15 sts as row 24 of chart, K3, P105, K3, work next 15 sts as row 24 of chart, K4, P1, K1.

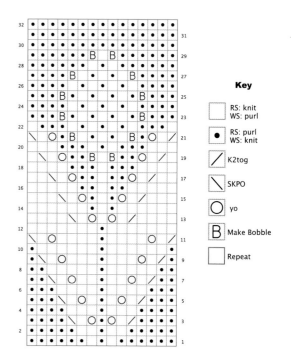

Key

☐	RS: knit WS: purl
●	RS: purl WS: knit
╱	K2tog
╲	SKPO
O	yo
B	Make Bobble
☐	Repeat

Row 25: K1, P1, K1, P3, work next 15 sts as row 25 of chart, P3, K105 sts, P3, work next 15 sts as row 25 of chart, P3, K1, P1, K1.

Row 26: K1, P1, K4, work next 15 sts as row 26 of chart, K3, P105, K3, work next 15 sts as row 26 of chart, K4, P1, K1.

Row 27: K1, P1, K1, P3, work next 15 sts as row 27 of chart, P3, K3, yo, K2tog, *K5, skpo, yo, K1, yo, K2tog, rep from * 8 times more, K5, skpo, yo, K3, P3, work next 15 sts as row 27 of chart, P3, K1, P1, K1.

Row 28: K1, P1, K4, work next 15 sts as row 28 of chart, K3, P105, K3, work next 15 sts as row 28 of chart, K4, P1, K1.

Row 29: K1, P1, K1, P3, work next 15 sts as row 29 of chart, P3 K2, (yo) twice, K2tog, yo, K2tog, *K3, skpo, yo, K1, (yo) twice, K2tog, yo, K2tog, rep from * 8 times more, K3, skpo, yo, K1, (yo) twice, K2tog, K1, P3, work next 15 sts as row 29 of chart, P3, K1, P1, K1.

Row 30: K1, P1, K4, work next 15 sts as row 30 of chart, K3, P105 dropping one strand of each double yo on previous row, K3, work next 15 sts as row 30 of chart, K4, P1, K1.

Row 31: K1, P1, K1, P3, work next 15 sts as row 31 of chart, P3, K3, yo, K2tog, *K5, skpo, yo, K1, yo, K2tog, rep from * 8 times more, K5, skpo, yo, K3, P3, work next 15 sts as row 31 of chart, P3, K1, P1, K1.

Row 32: K1, P1, K4, work next 15 sts as row 32 of chart, K3, P105, K3, work next 15 sts as row 32 of chart, K4, P1, K1. Rep these last 32 rows 5 times more, ending with RS facing for next row.

TOP BORDER

Row 1 (RS): K1, P1, K1, P3, *work next 15 sts as row 1 of chart, P3, rep from * to last 3 sts, K1, P1, K1.

Row 2: K1, P1, K4, *work next 15 sts as row 2 of chart, K3, rep from * to last 3 sts, K1, P1, K1. These last 2 rows place chart with 3 sts of seed (moss) stitch either end with 3 sts in rev st st between the charts. Cont as set until all 32 rows of chart have been completed, ending with RS facing for next row.

Row 33 (RS): K1, *P1, K1, rep from * to end.
Rep last row 3 times more, ending with RS facing for next row. BO in patt.

FINISHING

Block to measurements carefully following instructions on ball band.

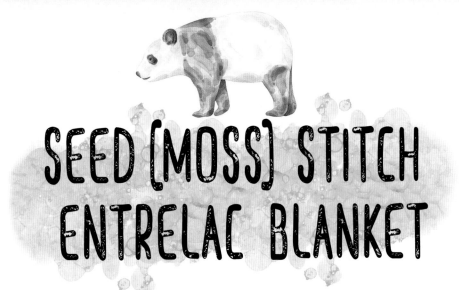

SEED (MOSS) STITCH ENTRELAC BLANKET

SIZE
Width (approx): 28 [31: 34 in (71 [79: 86] cm)
Length (approx): 36 [39: 42] in (91.5 [99: 107] cm)

ABBREVIATIONS
See inside front flap

SPECIAL ABBREVIATION
C4B slip next 2 sts onto CN and leave at back of work, K2, then K2 from CN

C4F slip next 2 sts onto CN and leave at front of work, K2, then K2 from CN

MATERIALS NEEDED
DMC Woolly (136 yd/125 m per 50g bal)
4 [5: 6] x balls of Light Grey (121) **A**
3 [4: 5] x balls of Dark Grey (122) **B**
US 6 (4 mm) needles
Cable needle

GAUGE (TENSION)
24 sts and 40 rows to 4 in (10 cm) measured over Seed (Moss) stitch using US 6 (4 mm) needles.

BLANKET

BASE TRIANGLES
Using US 6 (4 mm) needles and yarn **A** CO 112 [126: 140] sts **loosely.**

*Row 1 (WS): K1, P1, turn.

Row 2: P1, K1, turn.

Rows 3 and 4: K1, P1, K1, turn.

Row 5: (K1, P1) twice, turn.

Row 6: (P1, K1) twice, turn.

Rows 7 and 8: (K1, P1) twice, K1, turn.

Row 9: (K1, P1) 3 times, turn.

Row 10: (P1, K1) 3 times, turn.

Rows 11 and 12: (K1, P1) 3 times, K1, turn.

Row 13: (K1, P1) 4 times, turn.

Row 14: (P1, K1) 4 times, turn.

Rows 15 and 16: (K1, P1) 4 times, K1, turn.

Row 17: (K1, P1) 5 times, turn.

Row 18: (P1, K1) 5 times, turn.

Rows 19 and 20: (K1, P1) 5 times, K1, turn.

Row 21: (K1, P1) 6 times, turn.

Row 22: (P1, K1) 6 times, turn.

Rows 23 and 24: (K1, P1) 6 times, K1, turn.

Row 25: (K1, P1) 7 times, do not turn.
Rep from * for 7 [8: 9] more triangles - 8 [9:10] Base Triangles made. Turn.

RIGHT SIDE EDGE TRIANGLE

Using yarn **B**.

Row 1 (RS): K2, turn.

Row 2: K1, P1, turn.

Row 3: Inc in first st by working (K1, P1) into same st, skpo, turn.

Row 4: K1, P1, K1, turn.

Row 5: Inc in first st by working (P1, K1) into same st, P1, skpo, turn.

Row 6: (K1, P1) twice, turn.

Row 7: Inc in first st by working (K1, P1) into same st, K1, P1, skpo, turn.

Row 8: (K1, P1) twice, K1, turn.

Row 9: Inc in first st by working (P1, K1) into same st, P1, K1, P1, skpo, turn.

Row 10: (K1, P1) 3 times, turn.

Row 11: Inc in first st by working (K1, P1) into same st, (K1, P1) twice, skpo, turn.

Row 12: (K1, P1) 3 times, K1, turn.

Row 13: Inc in first st by working (P1, K1) into same st, (P1, K1) twice, P1, skpo, turn.

Row 14: (K1, P1) 4 times, turn.

Row 15: Inc in first st by working (K1, P1) into same st, (K1, P1) 3 times, skpo, turn.

Row 16: (K1, P1) 4 times, K1.

Row 17: Inc in first st by working (P1, K1) into same st, (P1, K1) 3 times, P1, skpo, turn.

Row 18: (K1, P1) 5 times, turn.

Row 19: Inc in first st by working (K1, P1) into same st, (K1, P1) 4 times, skpo, turn.

Row 20: (K1, P1) 5 times, K1, turn.

Row 21: Inc in first st by working (P1, K1) into same st, (P1, K1) 4 times, P1, skpo, turn.

Row 22: (K1, P1) 6 times, turn.

Row 23: Inc in first st by working (K1, P1) into same st, (K1, P1) 5 times, skpo, turn.

Row 24: (K1, P1) 6 times, K1.

Row 25: Inc in first st by working (P1, K1) into same st, (P1, K1) 5 times, P1, skpo, **do not turn**. Right Hand Triangle is completed. Leave these 14 sts on right needle.

RS RECTANGLES

Using yarn **B**.

*Next row (RS): Pick up and knit 14 sts evenly along edge of next triangle/rectangle, turn.

Row 1 and every foll alt row (WS): K1, P1, K1, P8, K1, P1, K1, turn.

Row 2: K1, P1, K10, P1, skpo (with last st of rectangle and first st of next triangle/rectangle), turn.

Row 4: K1, P1, K1, C4B, C4F, K1, P1, skpo (with last st of rectangle and first st of next triangle/rectangle), turn.

Row 6: As row 2.

Row 8: K1, P1, K1, C4F, C4B, K1, P1, skpo (with last st of rectangle and first st of next triangle/rectangle), turn.

Row 10: As row 2.

Row 12: As row 4.

Row 14: As row 2.

Row 16: As row 8.

Row 18: As row 2.

Row 20: As row 4.

Row 22: As row 2.

Row 24: As row 8.

Row 26: As row 2.

Row 28: K1, P1, K10, P1, skpo (with last st of rectangle and first st of next triangle/rectangle), do not turn.

Rep from * 6 [7: 8] times more - 7 [8: 9] RS Rectangles have been made. **Do not turn**.

LEFT SIDE EDGE TRIANGLE

Using yarn **B**.

Next row (RS): Pick up and knit 14 sts evenly along edge of last triangle/rectangle, turn.

Row 1 (WS): K2tog, (P1, K1) 6 times, turn.

Row 2: (K1, P1) 6 times, K1, turn.

Row 3: P2tog, (K1, P1) 5 times, K1, turn.

Row 4: (K1, P1) 6 times, turn.

Row 5: K2tog, (P1, K1) 5 times, turn.

Row 6: (K1, P1) 5 times, K1, turn.

Row 7: P2tog, (K1, P1) 4 times, K1, turn.

Row 8: (K1, P1) 5 times, turn.

Row 9: K2tog, (P1, K1) 4 times, turn.

Row 10: (K1, P1) 4 times, K1, turn.

Row 11: P2tog, (K1, P1) 3 times, K1, turn.

Row 12: (K1, P1) 4 times, turn.

Row 13: K2tog, (P1, K1) 3 times, turn.

Row 14: (K1, P1) 3 times, K1, turn.

Row 15: P2tog, (K1, P1) twice, K1, turn.

Row 16: (K1, P1) 3 times, turn.

Row 17: K2tog, (P1, K1) twice, turn.

Row 18: (K1, P1) twice, K1, turn.

Row 19: P2tog, K1, P1, K1, turn.

Row 20: (K1, P1) twice, turn.

Row 21: K2tog, P1, K1, turn.

Row 22: K1, P1, K1, turn.

Row 23: P2tog, K1, turn.

Row 24: K1, P1, turn.

Row 25: Using yarn **A** P2tog, (1 st on right needle), **do not turn.**

WS RECTANGLES

Using yarn **A**.

Next row (WS): Pick up and **purl** 13 sts evenly along edge of triangle just worked, turn.

*Row 1 (RS): P1, K1, P1, K8, P1, K1, P1, turn.

Row 2 and every foll alt row: P1, K1, P10, K1, P2tog (with last st of rectangle and first st of next triangle/rectangle), turn.

Row 3: As row 1.

Row 5: P1, K1, P1, C4B, C4F, P1, K1, P1, turn.

Row 7: As row 1.

Row 9: P1, K1, P1, C4F, C4B, P1, K1, P1, turn.

Row 11: As row 1.

Row 13: As row 5.

Row 15: As row 1.

Row 17: As row 9.

Row 19: As row 1.

Row 21: As row 5.

Row 23: As row 1.

Row 25: As row 9.

Row 27: As row 1.

Row 28: As row 2, do not turn.

Next row (WS): Pick up and **purl** 14 sts evenly along edge of next RS Rectangle, turn.

Rep from * 7 [8: 9] times more - 8 [9: 10] WS Rectangles have been made. Turn.

**Using yarn **B work 1 Right Side Edge Triangle.
Using yarn **B** work 1 row of RS Rectangles.
Using yarn **B** work 1 Left Side Edge Triangle.
Using yarn **A** work 1 row of WS Rectangles.
Rep from ** 5 [6: 7] times more.
Using yarn **B** work 1 Right Side Edge Triangle.
Using yarn **B** work 1 row of RS Rectangles.
Using yarn **B** work 1 Left Side Edge Triangle.

TOP TRIANGLES

Using yarn **A**.

*Next row (WS): Pick up and **purl** 13 sts evenly along edge of triangle just worked, turn.

Row 1 (RS): (P1, K1) 7 times, turn.

Row 2: P2tog, (K1, P1) 5 times, K1, P2tog, turn.

Row 3: (P1, K1) 6 times, P1, turn.

Row 4: K2tog, (P1, K1) 5 times, P2tog, turn.

Row 5: (P1, K1) 6 times, turn.
Row 6: P2tog, (K1, P1) 4times, K1, P2tog, turn.

Row 7: (P1, K1) 5 times, P1, turn.

Row 8: K2tog, (P1, K1) 4 times, P2tog, turn.

Row 9: (P1, K1) 5 times, turn.

Row 10: P2tog, (K1, P1) 3 times, K1, P2tog, turn.

Row 11: (P1, K1) 4 times, P1, turn.

Row 12: K2tog, (P1, K1) 3 times, P2tog, turn.

Row 13: (P1, K1) 4 times, turn.

Row 14: P2tog, (K1, P1) twice, K1, P2tog, turn.

Row 15: (P1, K1) 3 times, P1, turn.
Row 16: K2tog, (P1, K1) twice, P2tog, turn.

Row 17: (P1, K1) 3 times, turn.

Row 18: P2tog, K1, P1, K1, P2tog, turn.

Row 19: (P1, K1) twice, P1, turn.

Row 20: K2tog, P1, K1, P2tog, turn.

Row 21: (P1, K1) twice, turn.

Row 22: P2tog, K1, P2tog, turn.

Row 23: P1, K1, P1, turn.

Row 24: K2tog, P2tog, turn.

Row 25: P1, K1, turn.

Row 26: P4tog, (1 st on right needle), do not turn.
Rep from * 7 [8: 9] times more, picking up sts along edge of rectangle instead of triangle. - 8 [9: 10] Top Triangles have been made.
Fasten off rem st.

FINISHING

Block to measurements carefully following instructions on ball band.

BORDER

Using US 6 (4 mm) needles and yarn **A** CO 5 sts.

Row 1 (RS): K3, Kfb, K1. 6 sts.

Row 2 and every foll alt row: Knit.

Row 3: K4, Kfb, K1. 7 sts.

Row 5: K5, Kfb, K1. 8 sts.

Row 7: K6, Kfb, K1. 9 sts.

Row 9: K7, Kfb, K1. 10 sts.

Row 11: K8, Kfb, K1. 11 sts.

Row 13: K9, Kfb, K1. 12 sts.

Row 15: K10, Kfb, K1. 13 sts.

Row 16: BO 8 sts (1 st on right needle) K to end. 5 sts.

These 16 rows form patt.

Cont in patt until straight edge of border fits along outer edge of blanket (sewing as you go), easing around corners and ending with row 11 and WS facing for next row.
BO knitwise.

FINISHING

Join remainder of border to blanket edge, then join CO and BO edges together.

CABLED BLANKET

SIZE
Width (approx): 21 in (53 cm)
Length (approx): 27½ in (70 cm)

ABBREVIATIONS
See inside front flap

SPECIAL ABBREVIATION
Cr3R slip next st onto CN and leave at back of work, K2, then P1 from CN

Cr3L slip next 2 sts onto CN and leave at front of work, P1, then K2 from CN

C4B slip next 2 sts onto CN and leave at back of work, K2, then K2 from CN

C4F slip next 2 sts onto CN and leave at front of work, K2, then K2 from CN

Cr4R slip next 2 sts onto CN and leave at back of work, K2, then P2 from CN

Cr4L slip next 2 sts onto CN and leave at front of work, P2, then K2 from CN

MATERIALS NEEDED
DMC Woolly (136 yd/125 m per 50g ball)
6 x balls of Cream (003)
US 5 (3.75 mm) needles
US 6 (4 mm) needles
Cable needle

GAUGE (TENSION)
24 sts and 30 rows to 4 in (10 cm) measured over patt using US 6 (4 mm) needles.

BLANKET
Using US 5 (3.75 mm) needles CO 124 sts.
Working in g st for 23 rows, ending with **WS** facing for next row.
Change to US 6 (4 mm) needles.

Next row (WS): K12, (Pfb) twice, K2, (Pfb) 4 times, K2, (Pfb) twice, *K4, (Pfb) twice, rep from * 4 times, *K2, (Pfb) 4 times, K2, (Pfb) twice, rep from * 3 times, *K4, (Pfb) twice, rep from * 4 times, K2, (Pfb) 4 times, K2, (Pfb) twice, K12. 172 sts.

Row 1 (RS): K10, (P2, C4B) twice, C4F, P2, (C4B, P4) 4 times, C4B, P2, C4B, C4F, (P2, C4B) twice, (C4F, P2) twice, C4B, C4F, P2, C4F, P4, (C4B, P4) 3 times, C4F, P2, C4B, (C4F, P2) twice, K10.

Row 2: K12, P4, K2, P8, K2, (P4, K4) 4 times, (P4, K2, P8, K2) 3 times, (P4, K4) 4 times, P4, K2, P8, K2, P4, K12.

Row 3: K10, P2, K4, P2, K8, P2, K4, P3, Cr3R, (Cr4L, Cr4R) twice, Cr3L, P3, (K4, P2, K8, P2) 3 times, K4, P3, Cr3R, (Cr4L, Cr4R) twice, Cr3L, P3, K4, P2, K8, P2, K4, P2, K10.

Row 4: K12, P4, K2, P8, K2, P4, K3, P2, K3, P4, K4, P4, K3, P2, K3, (P4, K2, P8, K2) 3 times, P4, K3, P2, K3, P4, K4, P4, K3, P2, K3, P4, K2, P8, K2, P4, K12.

Row 5: K10, P2, C4B, P2, C4F, (C4B, P2) twice, Cr3R, P3, C4F, P4, C4F, P3, Cr3L, (P2, C4B, P2, C4F, C4B) twice, (P2, C4F) twice, C4B, P2, C4F, P2, Cr3R, P3, C4F, P4, C4F, P3, Cr3L, (P2, C4F) twice, C4B, P2, C4F, P2, K10.

Row 6: K12, P4, K2, P8, K2, P4, K2, P2, (K4, P4) twice, K4, P2, K2, (P4, K2, P8, K2) 3 times, P4, K2, P2, (K4, P4) twice, K4, P2, K2, P4, K2, P8, K2, P4, K12.

Row 7: K10, P2, K4, P2, K8, P2, K4, P2, K2, P3, Cr3R, Cr4L, Cr4R, Cr3L, P3, K2, P2, (K4, P2, K8, P2) 3 times, K4, P2, K2, P3, Cr3R, Cr4L, Cr4R, Cr3L, P3, K2, P2, K4, P2, K8, P2, K4, P2, K10.

Row 8: K12, P4, K2, P8, K2, P4, K2, (P2, K3) twice, P4, (K3, P2) twice, K2, (P4, K2, P8, K2) 3 times, P4, K2, (P2, K3) twice, P4, (K3, P2) twice, K2, P4, K2, P8, K2, P4, K12.

Row 9: K10, (P2, C4B) twice, C4F, P2, C4B, P2 (K2, P3) twice, C4B, (P3, K2) twice, (P2, C4B) twice, C4F, (P2, C4B) twice, (C4F, P2) twice, C4B, (C4F, P2) twice, (K2, P3) twice, C4B, (P3, K2) twice, P2, C4F, P2, C4B, (C4F, P2) twice, K10.

Row 10: As row 8.

Row 11: K10, P2, K4, P2, K8, P2, K4, P2, K2, P3, Cr3L, Cr4R, Cr4L, Cr3R, P3, K2, P2, (K4, P2, K8, P2) 3 times, K4, P2, K2, P3, Cr3L, Cr4R, Cr4L, Cr3R, P3, K2, P2, K4, P2, K8, P2, K4, P2, K10.

Row 12: As row 6.

Row 13: K10, P2, C4B, P2, C4F, (C4B, P2) twice, Cr3L, P3, C4F, P4, C4F, P3, Cr3R, (P2, C4B, P2, C4F, C4B) twice, (P2, C4F) twice, C4B, P2, C4F, P2, Cr3L, P3, C4F, P4, C4F, P3, Cr3R, (P2, C4F) twice, C4B, P2, C4F, P2, K10.

Row 14: As row 4.

Row 15: K10, P2, K4, P2, K8, P2, K4, P3, Cr3L, (Cr4R, Cr4L) twice, Cr3R, P3, (K4, P2, K8, P2) 3 times, K4, P3, Cr3L, (Cr4R, Cr4L) twice, Cr3R, P3, K4, P2, K8, P2, K4, P2, K10.

Row 16: As row 2.

Last 16 rows form patt.

Cont in patt until work meas approx 25 in (64 cm), ending after patt row 1 and **WS** facing for next row.

Change to US 5 (3.75 mm) needles.

Next row (WS): K12, (P2tog) twice, K2, (P2tog) 4 times, K2, (P2tog) twice, *K4, (P2tog) twice, rep from * 4 times, *K2, (P2tog) 4 times, K2, (P2tog) twice, rep from * 3 times, *K4, (P2tog) twice, rep from * 4 times, K2, (P2tog) 4 times, K2, (P2tog) twice, K12. 124 sts.

Work in g st for 23 rows, ending with **WS** facing for next row. BO knitwise (on **WS**).

FINISHING

Block to measurements carefully following instructions on ball band.

SIMPLE RIBBED BLANKET

SIZE
Width (approx): 23½ [28: 32¼] in (69 [74: 79] cm)
Length (approx): 30 [35: 40] in (80 [90: 100] cm)

ABBREVIATIONS
See inside front flap

MATERIALS NEEDED
DMC Woolly (136 yd/125 m per 50g ball)
5 [6: 8] x balls of Grey (124)
US 5 (3.75 mm) needles
US 6 (4 mm) needles

GAUGE (TENSION)
24 sts and 29 rows to 4 in (10 cm) measured over patt using US 6 (4 mm) needles.

BLANKET

Using US 5 (3.75 mm) needles CO 166 [178: 190] sts.
Work in g st for 12 [14: 16] rows, ending with RS facing for next row.
Change to US 6 (4 mm) needles.

Row 1 (RS): Knit.

Row 2: K6[7:8], P4, *K1, P4, rep from * to last 6[7:8] sts, K6[7:8].
These 2 rows form patt.
Cont in patt until work measures approx 30¼ [34: 37¾] in (77 [86.5: 96] cm), ending with row 2 of patt and RS facing for next row.

Change to US 5 (3.75 mm) needles.
Work in g st for 12 [14: 16] rows, ending with RS facing for next row. BO.

FINISHING
Block to measurements carefully following instructions on ball band.

LACY DIAMOND BLANKET

SIZE
Width (approx): 29 [31½: 34] in (74 [80: 86] cm)
Length (approx): 36½ [39½: 42¼] in (93 [100: 107] cm)

ABBREVIATIONS
See inside front flap

MATERIALS NEEDED
DMC Woolly (136 yd/125 m per 50g ball)
7 [8: 9] x balls of Cream (003)
US 5 (3.75 mm) needles
US 6 (4 mm) needles

GAUGE (TENSION)
22 sts and 29 rows to 4 in (10 cm) measured over patt using US 6 (4 mm) needles.

BLANKET

Using US 5 (3.75 mm) needles CO 163 [175: 187] sts.
Work in g st for 6 rows, ending with RS facing for next row.
Change to US 6 (4 mm) needles.

Row 1 (RS): K4, *yo, skpo, K7, K2tog, yo, K1, rep from * to last 3 sts, K3.

Row 2 and every foll alt row: K3, P to last 3 sts, K3.

Row 3: K4, *K1, yo, skpo, K5, K2tog, yo, K2, rep from * to last 3 sts, K3.

Row 5: K4, *(yo, skpo) twice, K3, (K2tog, yo) twice, K1, rep from * to last 3 sts, K3.

Row 7: K4, *K1, (yo, skpo) twice, K1, (K2tog, yo) twice, K2, rep from * to last 3 sts, K3.

Row 9: K4, *(yo, skpo) twice, yo, sl 1, K2tog, psso, yo, (K2tog, yo) twice, K1, rep from * to last 3 sts, K3.

Row 11: K4, *K3, K2tog, yo, K1, yo, skpo, K4, rep from * to last 3 sts, K3.

Row 13: K4, *K2, K2tog, yo, K3, yo, skpo, K3, rep from * to last 3 sts, K3.

Row 15: K4, *K1, (K2tog, yo) twice, K1, (yo, skpo) twice, K2, rep from * to last 3 sts, K3.

Row 17: K4, *(K2tog, yo) twice, K3, (yo, skpo) twice, K1, rep from * to last 3 sts, K3.

Row 19: K3, K2tog, *(yo, K2tog) twice, yo, K1, (yo, skpo) twice, yo, sl 1, K2tog, psso, rep from * to last 14 sts, (yo, K2tog) twice, yo, K1, (yo, skpo) 3 times, K3.

Row 20: K3, P to last 3 sts, K3.
These 20 rows form patt.
Rep the last 20 rows 12 [13: 14] times more, ending with RS facing for next row.
Change to US 5 (3.75 mm) needles.
Work in g st for 6 rows, ending with RS facing for next row.
BO.

FINISHING

Block to measurements carefully following instructions on ball band.

ABBREVIATIONS

K	knit
P	purl
CO	cast on
BO	bind (cast) off
st(s)	stitch(es)
inc	increas(e)(ing)
dec	decreas(e)(ing)
Kfb	knit into front then back of next stitch
st st	stockinette (stocking) stitch (1 row K, 1 row P)
g st	garter stitch (K every row)
Beg	begin(ning)
foll	following
folls	follows
rem	remain(ing)
rep	repeat
alt	alternate
cont	continue
patt	pattern
tog	together
mm	millimeters
cm	centimeter(s)
in	inch(es)
m	meter(s)
yd	yard(s)
g	gram(s)
oz	ounce(s)
RS	right side
WS	wrong side
sl 1	slip one stitch
psso	pass slipped stitch over
p2sso	pass 2 slipped stitches over
skpo	slip 1, K1, pass slipped stitch over
tbl	through back loop(s)
yo	yarn over
cn	cable needle
meas	measures
0	no stitches, times or rows
-	no stitches, times or rows for that size
M1	make one stitch by picking up horizontal loop before next stitch and knitting into back of it
M1P	make one stitch by picking up horizontal loop before next stitch and purling into back of it

About the Author

Jody Long was born in Portsmouth, in the United Kingdom. He grew up in Waterlooville, Hampshire, and moved to Málaga, Spain, in 2014. For over twelve years, he designed for all the major U.K. and U.S. knitting magazines, then moved on to design for knitting mills around the globe and writing knitting books. Jody has also designed for celebrity clients.

Jody has a website which is www.jodylongknits.com

JodyLongKnits
JodyLongKnits
JodyLongKnits

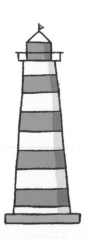